# the ripening

## Nancy London

Essays on Love, Loss, Marriage and Aging

Safe Place Publishing
ISBN 979-8-218-30045-6

All rights reserved. No portion of this book may be reproduced, stored in a retrieval system, or transmitted in any form or by any means, mechanical, electronic, no photocopying, recording, or otherwise, without written permission from the publisher.

**THE RIPENING  Essays on Love, Loss, Marriage and Aging**
copyright ©2024 Nancy London
by Nancy London. All rights reserved.

Book design by Limor Farber Design Studio

For Richard, my north star
For my ancestors, who crossed time and tide
to bring me their blessings,
and for my mother.

There is no end to love.
We may tear ourselves away,
or fall off the cliff we thought sacred,
or return one day to find the home we dreamt of burning.
But when the rain slows to a slant
and the pavement turns cold,
that place where I keep you and you and all of you -
that place opens, like a fist no longer strong enough
to stay closed.

— Mark Nepo



--And did you get what
you wanted from this life, even so?
I did.
And what did you want?
To call myself beloved, to feel myself
beloved on the earth.

— Raymond Carver

# Contents

Prologue...................................................15

## Part One | Seed

Sing Back the Light.................................21
Our Broken Hallelujah...........................25
Gypsy and Thief.....................................29
Daddy's Girl ...........................................33
Firefly Angels..........................................37
Shelter From the Storm .........................43
Black Russians and Village Bars............47
Erotica......................................................49
Stealing to Save My Life .......................53
The History Dogs Are Barking ............57
Hunger ....................................................61
The Voice of the Wound.......................65
Where I Found You ...............................69
Breast Stroking Home............................71
Speak, Silence.........................................75

## Part Two | Water

| | |
|---|---:|
| KNOCK KNOCK JOKE | 81 |
| ROCK AND ROLL | 87 |
| SOFT CANDIES AND HARD WHISKEY | 91 |
| MAGIC MUSHROOMS | 97 |
| MERMAID | 103 |
| HANDS ON | 109 |
| HOT SEAT | 113 |
| MANTRA ON REPEAT | 117 |
| THE HOUR OF THE BLACK DOG | 119 |
| LOVE NOT LOVE | 123 |
| WILD STRAWBERRIES | 127 |
| WHAT COURAGE SAID | 131 |
| LSD WITH BUDDHA | 135 |
| WE HOLD HANDS AND JUMP | 143 |

## Part Three | Bloom

| | |
|---|---|
| Borderlands | 151 |
| Holy Holy | 155 |
| Across the Universe | 157 |
| And Then There Was Fear | 161 |
| Addictions | 165 |
| Unchained Melody | 169 |
| Home | 173 |
| Dialogue With Our Dreams | 179 |
| Enemies | 183 |
| Besotted and Bedazzled | 187 |
| Small Deaths | 193 |
| Mama Said There'd Be Days Like This | 197 |
| Breasts | 201 |
| Beauty Stepped into the Room | 205 |
| Dreamtime | 209 |
| Love's Wounds | 213 |

## Part Four | Ripen

| | |
|---|---|
| INITIATION | 219 |
| LOVE LETTERS | 223 |
| THE HISTORY OF LOVE | 227 |
| WILD RIDE | 231 |
| WORD SALAD | 235 |
| WEARY WARRIOR | 239 |
| CHERISH EVERY STUPID MOMENT | 243 |
| SLOWER, FUNNIER, WISER | 247 |
| THE NEW STORY | 251 |
| SANCTUARY | 255 |
| DANCING TO THE END OF TIME | 259 |
| PRAYERS FOR THE DEAD | 263 |

## Part Five | Harvest

TIME AND THE RIVER.......................... 269
NO MORE FIXING ............................... 273
I WISH SOMEONE HAD TOLD ME................... 277

EPILOGUE: OLD AGE COMES HAPPY ........... 281

Nancy London

# The Ripening | Prologue

LISTEN. I WAS SPRINGTIME. I was the color green shooting up from the ground - new life, new maiden, exploding star roaming in search of who knows what and it did not matter, hopping trains hitching ditching wandering, spreading honey like lust and lust like life itself.

Listen. I was the peach of summer, so ripe the juice ran down my arm, so sticky sweet the bees came to me humming. I was watermelon, red as passion, slick as sex on a hot summer night. I was what quenched your thirst crossing the desert. I was an all-white bikini with sun kissed skin.

Listen. I was salsa dancing. I was the feather and the fan and the audience cheering for more. I was the castanets and the wild parrots mating.

I was a symphony, an opera, an outdoor concert with everyone shouting *hell yes* and *now* and *always* and *more* and now Listen. Now I am a piano solo at midnight in the minor chords my ancestors chanted in the temples, the ones that were destroyed, burned, bombed, turned to ash and bone.

Now I am autumn. The pear ripening on the windowsill. The green apple baking in the pie. Now I am home and in my garden. I make an altar from the rocks and shells I gather. This is enough for now. Now I am yoga, long and slow and solitary on my mat. Corpse pose but not dead yet, I laugh quietly to myself. Not nearly dead yet.

Listen. I was spring and summer and planting seeds and watering them, breasts filled with milk for a hungry baby who could never get enough and now I have the scars from the woman's plague that carved my breast open and left me sore and sometimes scared that it will circle back around and call for me again.

Listen. There was only one friend who knew how many cowboys and gypsy thieves I had loved. The number so funny, so large, so holy shit really? We pinkie swore to keep each other's secrets until death do us part.

And now Listen. I have been married to one man for 36 years. I have put this part of my summer away in the steamer trunk so that I might be wholly his. Sex is not like it used to be, fast and hot and anywhere any time. Now I am perfumed and oiled, and through the electric shock of orgasm remember that the gods intended sex to be a portal to the divine.

Listen. I am autumn, harvesting what I planted. The pumpkins and winter squash, the sage and rosemary, everything drying and ready for the season of change and transformation.

Winter is coming. This is not a new story.

Listen. I am getting ready. I'm bargaining with winter, saying give me more time.

Give me the wisdom to greet you with full hearted acceptance.

Teach me to carry grief in one hand and gratitude in the other.

Let grief keep my heart undefended, open to the sorrow of others, and let the place inside where it is unbreakable be where we meet in compassion for each other, where what is left beyond this time of aging skin and softening muscle is radiance and laughter.

There is no time left to hesitate or hold back.

Crack open my heart and scatter my seeds on the wind, each one a rose blooming in the fragrant garden of healing and forgiveness. Hear the soft hum of my prayer: when winter comes silently, her white light blinding, I will have been ripened in the service of love.

Listen.

# Part One

## SEED

Nancy London

# Sing Back the Light

SHE WOKE ME WITH the gentle touch of a feather across my face.

Get up, she whispered. It's the dark times. We have work to do.

I resisted. I was tired. You got that right, I said. These are the dark times. I need coffee.

She followed me into the kitchen and that's when I noticed her wings.

Ok, I said. Who exactly are you again?

She sat and waited for me to stir milk and honey into my cup, drink, come awake.

We need your help, she said, ignoring my question. To bring back the light. Dark and light are poised in equal balance, she said. Our job is to make prayers, offerings, to coax the light back from the place of darkness.

So wait. You want my help to do what?

I want you to help us bring back the light.

I laughed. Things have been a little dark for me too,

I said. Not sure how much help I can be. Are you sure you came to the right address?

She smiled. I'm sure.

It's not hard, she said, but it's not exactly easy, either. It means you offer yourself to a world in need. Offer what you can promise as a token to the light that needs coaxing. You know, courting…like a love song.

I cleared my throat. Ok, ok. Dear Light, I began, feeling foolish. I see that you have retreated into darkness, and honestly, who can blame you. I'm not sure what I have to offer, being just one small person, but here goes.

I pledge myself to kindness, which really is harder than it sounds. I offer my patience to those who come to me for comfort, even when I am too busy and want to turn them away.

How am I doing?

Just fine, she said.

I promise to remember the extinct ones of air and water and earth. I promise to sing their names so that my children and their children will know how they once flew and swam and roamed in freedom and in beauty.

Go on, she prompted.

I offer my willingness to be vulnerable to those I love. To say I was wrong, I'm sorry, please forgive me.

I offer myself to the gods of creativity and ask that

I not waste any impulse to share what I make out of false modesty.

I offer my prayers to the ones no one prays for - the voiceless, the homeless. The lonely, the broken.

I was suddenly wide awake.

She took me to the edge of the universe and showed me where light and dark stood in perfect balance, where time stopped, where the chaotic gaping void threatened to engulf the light. It was cold and she wrapped me in her wings.

Within each of us, she said, is an inner sun that is needed to call back the light from the extremes of darkness in the world. We are being asked to assist in the renewal of life, to bring back the light of spirit from the far reaches of a devouring abyss.

But I feel small and frail, I said. I don't know how.

Start by nourishing happiness in order to handle grief, she said. Light a candle. Let it grow into a bonfire. Throw into it all false ideas of your smallness, your limitations that no longer serve you. Grow your light from the radiance of the flames. Dare to become who you are meant to be. Ignite your inner joy and let your sense of self become a beacon for others.

Let the spark that is your own radiance start the fire that becomes the flame that beats the drum that calls up

the winds that bring down the rains that paints the sky that restores the holy hallelujah in the midst of darkness.
   Sing yes, she said.
   Sing now.
   Sing the song of grace and surrender.
   Sing for what we can't yet name, but is on the horizon.
   Breathe, she said.  Bloom, she said. Blaze.

# Our Broken Hallelujah

NOVEMBER 1ST Day of the Dead.

My ancestors are waiting at the gate, dressed in heavy winter coats with a dusting of snow on the collar. The air smells of ancient Ukrainian pine forests and clean running streams. I coax them in and they sit, pull off their gloves, warm their hands by the fire then throw back the shot glasses of vodka I have left for them on my altar.

I'm so glad to see you, I say. It's been a rough year.

My grandmother beckons me to her. Sit, *Maideleh*, she says. Tell me what troubles you. She tucks a strand of hair behind my ear and I catch her familiar scent: wild stormy seas and the sorrows that cling to her like a well-worn sweater. I tell her my friends have headaches or stomach aches, can't sleep or have started drinking again. We are half out of our minds with grief over the daily atrocities - the tweets and rants, the rape of our daughters and of our earth with impunity, with entitlement.

Child, *darlinka*, she croons. You want to know how

we survived? We had faith. And when our faith ran out, we had each other. We lit candles on Friday nights and said *thank you, thank you* for each small blessing. We knew that kindness built community, that it was the fabric that wove the web that sustained us. We grew food and medicinal herbs and shared them. We made alliances that crossed political barriers and we grew strong. We tore down walls. Toppled governments everyone said were too big to fail.

I do not mean to make it sound easy. I mean to say we did it.

We learned to share our bread and what water we had left, because without this kindness there is no hope for peace, without this reaching out to the other saying you and I - we are the same. You are the me I have been exiling. You are the part of me I have been looking for, the stranger with the dark eyes. You are the beloved, the mother, the son, the daughter. Come and share what I have because if you starve I starve too, and if you go thirsty my mouth is also dry.

We are asking you to keep our stories alive. Under the skin and bone of your DNA lies the dark mystery of your inheritance. We are here to tell you that you already have within you all the brilliance, power and beauty needed to restore your world. We've passed down resiliency, intuition, generosity, cooperation, empathy, humor, self-reliance. Vision and imagination. The capacity for joy. Courage even when you are afraid. We have given you everything you need to survive.

We are asking you to believe that your love is enough, that forgiveness is possible, and that you are here to add the rhythm section of your heart to the garage band tuning up to the ecstatic chords of *yes* and *yes* and the holy refrain of *thank you*.

We ask you to imagine that your imperfect love is perfect. To imagine that when you rise mute and disheartened, weighed down by despair, you knock on the door of your heart and say - *Get up honey. It's time to put your red dress on.* Time to add your song, your dance, your heartbeat to the gathering at the edge of the forest, at all the fast running waters, at the center of the center of your life. To believe that your love, your broken hallelujah, is exactly what the world needs now.

Our ancestors are gesturing to us from over the gate today, tossing hard candies to get our attention, poking each other in the ribs, laughing, telling bawdy jokes. Invite them in with roses and wine and their favorite accordion music. Take the seeds they offer and plant them in the tangle and promise of the world waiting to bloom. Make them their favorite soup. Ask to hear again the old tales we have almost forgotten. About the village innocent who outwits the bully; the buried treasure and where the map is to be found. About the wolf and the bear who know the way home. About the unseen forces that arrive when we call for them.

Our ancestors are here to bless us with the living waters of their grief and their joy. They are here to remind us that love never fails.

# Gypsy and Thief

THERE'S NO WAY TO WRITE about my ancestors without beginning with my legs, the same legs I inherited from my mother, from my grandmother before her, and probably from my Ukrainian great-grandmother, although in the only photo I have of her, she's seated with her hands folded neatly in her lap.

I've named these legs Gypsy and Thief because they knew when to run and where to hide, how to stay one step ahead, to negotiate, to bend the truth, to leave the game with the winnings tucked deep inside a boot. These legs traveled the road of the nomad, the wanderer, the one who never settled, who grabbed what was needed and ducked fast into shadow.

My legs testify to a long chain of ancestors back to that first awakening in Africa. Stretch. Move. Plant feet on the hot earth. Set a course north through the desert, eating the fat dates hanging down from trees, ripe as nipples, and then across the Red sea. Move on. Cross the Caucasus, up the Russian steppes and down into Odessa, Polynya and Kyiv. Feel how wet and fertile the soil is. Make plans, make a home, make love, make babies. Bury husbands. Make time to build community, gather herbs, brew medicines. Barefoot, legs so fucking sturdy they could lift a calf. Broad feet planted on the earth, a flag of defiance, toes burrowing, each one a stake in the ground. This is mine. Come any closer and I'll shoot you.

So what does this have to do with me, these legs that have run behind me for generations calling…Wait! Don't forget us! You need us!

Need you for what? I sneer, getting ready to curl my bangs before the high school prom. Fuck off. I'm washing my feet and putting on five inch heels.

You'll be sorry, they echo down the long corridor of my dreams.

No I won't, I yell back over my shoulder.

But still. Why do those legs want me to slip mine into their tough skin, their wrinkled flesh? So I stop and say…okay. You have five minutes. Spill.

And they say, first darling, sit down and have something cool to drink. Flex your little toesies. Remember this little piggy went to market?

I roll my eyes.

Please, I say. Why do you haunt me, follow me, bust my long limbed fantasy with a Yiddish- speaking ancestor I never knew?

Because, *Shaina Maidelah,* who do you think gave you your strength? How did you learn to stand your ground and hit back when your mother, may her soul rest in peace, felt free and happy to whack you across the mouth? How did you stand steady and fight back? Think about it. And how, if you don't mind me asking, did you walk out of the house and never look back? Certainly not on your hands, darling girl. And the moving from place to place, restless, pacing, running. How did you manage that? Right. On your Ukrainian legs. And when the ocean tried to drown you, the power of your kick against the swirling rip tide is what brought you to shore. And need I remind you of birthing your daughter, standing on your two beautiful pillars, pushing and grunting.

We have crossed deserts, bargained for food by spreading our legs, then closed them when it was time to leave. We have bent in prayer, in sorrow, left our tears to water the ground where we passed and could not settle, used our legs to jump from second story windows, flee the burning village, the synagogue in flames, used them to run, and run faster, as if our life depended on it. And it did.

And now? Now you lay your legs across the lap of your beloved and he rubs your feet. This little piggy went to market. This little piggy stayed at home.

THE RIPENING | Seed

# Daddy's Girl

My father skated on the black ice of heaven in between the goalposts of the stars, whistling as he tossed his hat onto the milky way, scooping up his daughter, his baby girl, swinging her gently in his arms, pressing her close to his beating heart that she might stay warm during the long cold nights of her mother's reign.

His smile warmed the weary, his brown eyes the color of *you can trust me,* his tall frame in three piece suits with white starched shirts. And did I mention cufflinks? And did I mention the fedora he wore that looked so like Bogey beckoning to Bacall. Beckoning the celebrated girl-child born under the sun's own sign, skin so golden, hair so fair, green eyes the color of sea glass and a laugh that opened the tight buds of springtime.

His wing was where I took shelter when the storms that were my mother raged, his whistle, the call I could hear across the frozen miles where she exiled me in my small room for my fairy tale beauty and my joy. And did

I mention the meals she prepared that did not settle so that I wrapped my arms around the cold white porcelain bowl and heaved and heaved until I was as empty of her as a child knew how to be.

But he and I had our ways. We met in the ocean where he taught me to dive under huge waves, safe as a clam as they rolled above my head, popping up into the spray, laughing. We met in front of the piano where I picked out show tunes that he sang for me, *My Little Girl* from Oklahoma, *People Will Say We're in Love*.

And they did. The relatives descended and ripped us apart. Shamed and blamed him. Sent me upstairs where I could still hear the accusations. *What do you think you're doing? You touch her too much. You fondle her. Your hands are always on her* and *that's what I've been trying to tell you,* shrieked the mother and then silence.

No more whistling or ducking waves, no show tunes, no long nights skating between the stars.

What did I do? I turned away from the sun, found sweetness in sugar, grew fat until I smelled like spoiled meat. Hid myself away. What had I done? Was I *bad sad mad glad?* None of the pictures the doctor showed me on the charts matched *devastated shocked despairing grieving betrayed.* None of them showed the slow progression of freezing, closing up shop, hanging the I am

Not At Home sign off the doorway to my heart.

My father placed me on an ice floe and sent me out to sea. He gave me a blanket and some chocolate and a salute as he set me adrift. I had neither oars nor a compass. No flashlight, no whistle. I froze. Ice formed under my fingernails and between my toes. Ice turned the tears on my eyelashes into tiny wind chimes. Ice was what I sucked on when the water ran out. Ice was what felt like heat if I thought about it hard enough.

I drifted. No way to signal back home. There was no shore, no green, just moonlight and ice and the feel of my heart stuttering underneath my frozen hand. I transformed into the Ice Queen. I grew a flipper and could navigate the frigid seas. I learned how to breathe underwater, and in time, I learned how to forget.

And then he died. Sudden, irreversible, no CPR needed. A massive heart attack.

They peeled off his watch and ring in the emergency room, passed them over to my mother. She gave my brother the watch. I gave the diamond ring away years later on my first acid trip in London to a homeless boy who looked hungry.

I did not attend the funeral. I stayed behind, polished my nails, ate a pint of chocolate ice cream standing up, spoon in spoon out, with the freezer door open.

Can I say that when my father died I was left with a hollow grief that still rings like a monastery bell calling me to prayer? The sound of footsteps in the snow, the winter birds with their small chests exploding in a hurrah of feathers trying to keep warm.

Can I say that I was never warm again? That the damp chill he left behind settled in my lungs and I try to cough it out every morning as I follow that call to prayer.

Can I say that I am burdened with the grief of missing him, the phantom dark-eyed lover, calling me deeper and deeper into the forest to find him gone, not where I thought he'd be, not anywhere at all, really. And can I say that I am grieving for someone who left too soon, someone who still whistles for me when the moon is full and the coyotes are out howling. Someone who tried to leave a breadcrumb trail, but here in the high desert, the crows always get to it first.

THE RIPENING | Seed

# Firefly Angels

IT WAS THE LAST DAY of sixth grade, late June, hot night. The fireflies I had captured at dusk were lighting up and banging against the side of the jar by my bed. My beautiful young parents were at a country club party - she in a Cinderella blue gown, he in a tuxedo with a red carnation in his lapel.

I woke to the air - shattering sound of my mother's high pitched wailing, retching, coughing. My mother trying to catch her breath.

I heard my heart beating in my ears. I heard all the other couples who should have been at the party murmuring below me.

I crept down the stairs. Past the men smoking cigars, that musty male smell, that *I'm in charge* smell my uncles gave off, and I wanted to huddle inside that smell, breathe its promise of safety but I could tell there was no safety to be had in that room. The smell of my own sweat.

I stood unnoticed, everyone sheltering my mother like tall trees bending where she had fallen. They brought her brandy. The sound of liquid pouring over ice in the squat clear glass.

I did not see my father.

I was getting cold but I couldn't move. Where would I go? Into the living room to sit silently and listen to my mother wail? Watch her collapse and scream for her husband, tear her hair, rip her beautiful Cinderella gown, drink brandy after brandy?

Would I crawl into the lap of my uncle? Ask him to rock me, to tell me very very very very very slowly where my daddy was?

I needed to go upstairs and hold tight to the jar of fireflies because I needed all the luck I could gather into my small hands, all the blessings I could beg from the firefly angels, all the good wishes I could ask from a God I suddenly believed in, desperately needed to see, to feel, to hear. Now was the moment to have the clock slow, the air freeze, the good will of all the guardians gather at my side and comfort me while I waited to hear where my daddy was.

Death came and sat on the edge of my bed. So quiet, so still, dressed all in gray shadows.

Your father is dead, she said. I could still hear the commotion downstairs, my mother keening, the aunts and uncles murmuring like a hive of bees. Tires screeching outside on wet pavement.

They'll lie to you for a bit, she said. They'll tell you he's sick. They'll say he's in the hospital, but he's dead.

I had been crying, but now I put down the jar of fireflies, took the tissue she offered and blew my nose.

I'm sorry, she said.

I smelled her then, a cold wind blowing down from the arctic, clean, sea swept, barren.

She let me cry some more, then said, I don't mean to rush you, but we have a lot of ground to cover before they come to tell you the truth.

I blew my nose again, sat up to listen.

You are so young, she said. It is such a hard time to lose the one you love so much.

I cried again while she sat perfectly still, waiting until I could compose myself.

I'm cold, I said.

She nodded. Of course you are, and I'm sorry that I cannot warm you. She placed one finger tip on my arm and the ice of the North beat through her pulse.

But, she said, I have sisters. And then five more women crowded into my small pink bedroom, a twelve year old's room with the last of my stuffed animals and the first of my bras and makeup.

This is my sister Life, she said. We were born conjoined and only through a great effort were we able to separate ourselves. Life smiled and warmed me with a shawl made from sunshine and praise.

And this, Death said, is my sister Sorrow. Sorrow bowed her head in greeting and spoke in a whisper. I will always be with you, she said, even when she – and here she nodded to the sister radiant in gold - even when Joy has come to dress you.

And I'm Grief, said the one who wept quietly in the corner. Sorrow and I will walk with you, and for a while we will pick out your friends and lovers, the ones who can hold you while you mourn.

But, said Joy, embracing her nearly transparent sister Happiness, she and I are never apart. We follow Sorrow when she weeps and Grief when she wails.

And now Life surrounded us all with a green glowing light and led me to the window. We will always be with you, she said. But for now Sorrow and Grief will have their way with you because that is how you will heal.

Despite the times of darkness when you will turn away from me and curse the rising sun, you will find your way back to Life and to the gifts that come only through a broken heart. Call for me and I will come and bless the wounds that cut so deep you think you will not survive.

I did not understand. I was too young to understand how I might come to find a gift within the grief that was crushing me.

Life handed me the jar of fireflies. This is how you begin, she said. You open the lid and surrender what you thought you could keep. You kneel in front of the rising moon and make an offering of what you hold dear.

Let them go, she said. Watch their lights blink on and off in the evening sky until the very last of their glow is absorbed into the night, and let us hold you until dawn, when the rest of your journey will begin.

Nancy London

# Shelter From the Storm

THERE WERE NEVER ANY storms as violent or unpredictable as my mother's.

Ice storms that froze me solid to the spot, that left me helpless until I taught myself how to thaw. Rain storms that drenched me to the bone, thunder that drove me to seek shelter inside my small room with the single bed and the weeping willow tree sighing against the window.

But oh there never was a pause in a storm as welcoming as hers. Double rainbows, roses in bloom. Silly girl talk and manicures. The time we watched a beauty pageant together, laughing, trash talking the outfits, gin and tonics, salted peanuts and flowered paper cocktail napkins. Mom already old, with her small round head of gray hair, half blind from macular degeneration, insisting that with the right makeup and costume she could look like that too.

Or the time we took the subway into the city, just the

two of us, to see Porgy and Bess. How *Summertime* was the song she sang. Low and throaty while she washed the dishes. How I stood by her side, wiping them dry, spellbound by the yearning in her voice. I'd be lulled into contentment and forget to check the barometer, caught suddenly in the flash flood downpour of her bottomless grief, her bitter tears wetting the cross-stitch tablecloth she might have set out for tea.

Sometimes a wind no one could have predicted rose up as my mother turned from the stove where she was stirring Uncle Ben's Converted White Rice. Then she would blow the hot fires of rage into the room until it scorched everything it touched.

I grew wise. I learned the number to dial for a weather report, but the satellite only told me it was coming. Then I would wet my finger and stick it up in the air to get the latest download.

*Folks, it's going to be a glorious morning, but by the afternoon a storm is rolling in, so take shelter.*

And I did. I created a safe place in my small bedroom with the pink rose wallpaper. Three Musketeer bars and Archie comics stolen from the corner candy store and stuffed to the back of my sock drawer. My radio and my diary, in case this storm turned out to be the 40-day kind.

Her storms left driftwood, green sea glass, the rotting wing of a bird tangled up in seaweed, all washed up exhausted onto the shore. Treasures to pick through. The sea glass on my narrow windowsill catching the morning light.

But it was the driftwood I hunted, brought home and washed clean, added to the growing pile of materials I was gathering to build the ark I would need to sail away. No compass, just the stars and the pull of my own true heart to deliver me to a shore where the weather was gentler, more predictable. A climate better suited to my soul.

Nancy London

# Black Russians and Village Bars

THE PLACE WHERE I WAS BORN grew my body like the workmen here in the desert layering mud on adobe walls. The city grew me like a cactus, gave me spines to protect me.

The city was tall buildings like shark teeth biting the sky, the smell of roasting chestnuts, hot pretzels, the sweat of police horses too long in the sun.

The city dressed me in black leather, gave me a Harley to ride.

The city was bars in the Village with lowlights and sawdust on the floors, with bartenders who glanced at my phony ID like it was Monopoly money, but still poured a twelve-year-old a whiskey with a wink. And the men who asked how old I was, and when I told them, laughed like I was a contestant on a quiz show and had just blown my stash.

The city fed me rhythm and harmony, the shuffle of feet, the way the tires sucked the street after a rain, a long slow kiss, rubber meets the road.

The city gave me a jungle with hot breath and coal black eyes behind the swinging vines.

The city gave me mother's milk in my Black Russians, poison in my pizzas, rot gut in my coffee, all to grow me up tough.

The city slapped me around. *Get up kid* it said. *No one ever said things would be fair; no one ever said there's a free lunch. Get up and fight back kid.*

The city gave me fire and ice like a one-two punch. Don't get too close or I'll burn you. Climb over the wall and I'll turn you to stone.

The city drew its map on my skin like a Japanese tattoo. Here the rose struggling to bloom. Here the ocean lapping at my toes. The constellation Weeping Girl inked across my chest.

The city left the lights on downtown where I shoplifted all my clothes. Left the lights on at the opera, at the foreign cinema, at the cafeteria, at the skating rink where I opened my mouth and swallowed the snow.

The city left the porch light on so I could fish out my keys, a fish out of water when I stumbled home from bus and subway, stepping over old men puking.

The city gave me cab fare, tucked me in and turned out the light, whispered *you're still a girl, you're still a child. But don't worry kid. I'll be back for you tomorrow.*

# Erotica

WHAT DO YOU CALL IT WHEN your brain goes offline and another body part takes over? When the pulse and thrust of something you are too young to name grabs you by the wrist and pulls you onto the dance floor. Puts two quarters into the jukebox with Janis on repeat - says *kick off your shoes and stay a while.* Says *what will you have to drink?* Says *don't worry, I'll get you home on time,* but never does.

What do you call it when the body always smells like something that has been born in the sea, when it's always wet between your legs, when all you can think about is slipping your hand down there and rubbing, because something is fizzing and blooming and shooting out into darkest space, and it is so beyond good and evil it makes you laugh out loud.

What do you call it when your boyfriend wants to lean you up against the brick wall behind your house and do the same thing to you - slip his finger inside your wet and hot, rub something you have no word for, did not know you could even share like that, did not know you could make a sound like dying, like pleasure, like please, again.

What do you call it when you are so young but old enough to want to lie on the cracked vinyl front seat of an old Chevrolet and give everything to your eighteen-year-old boyfriend because this is what feels good, this is pleasure, and in the dark time of those years, finding pleasure was the same as finding life, staking a claim on living, on joy, on the hallelujah release of the body into pure light.

I wanted it in the back seat of cars, up against bathroom walls while their wives poached salmon in the kitchen. I had no resistance to the pull, the musky smell these boy-men gave off, the tee shirt left on the floor that I wore to bed and remembered how the dark had embraced me, liberated, seduced and validated me. How these boys whose names and faces I have forgotten whispered dirty words as I came and woke me to my passion, held the key to the chains that bound me to my past, knew how to use their boot to kick down the door of my last resistance, lock their mouths onto any part of me, drag me by my hair into the pulse of my own desires.

## THE RIPENING | Seed

And then I learned what to call it. Sex. Fucking. Pussy. But that all came later and never fit just right, never described exactly what it felt like to have his hand reach down through my clothes and hunt through my thicket of hair for the wet, for the opening, for the pressure and rhythm that exploded me into another realm where light shimmered and the planets hummed, where kindness was the coin of the realm, where everything was forgiven with nothing to forgive, with everyone saying *I'm sorry* and *please let me help you* and *I won't do that again*. Where for those moments the rhythm of my hips moved me out of the dark alleys of my mind into a place I would hunt out again and again.

I learned to call it sex, but honey, in the beginning it was bliss. It was my ticket out of sorrow. It was my passport out of hell.

Nancy London

# Stealing to Save My Life

STEALING WAS THE ONLY WAY I knew how to get what I wanted before I even knew what I wanted. Candy, comic books, eyeshadow, nail polish, all stolen from the corner drugstore and stashed at the back of my sock drawer.

I was fat, a never - ending source of shame and outrage for Mom, which meant no allowance and by extension no money to buy candy, so I panhandled in the lobby of the Saturday afternoon movie theater. *Please ma'am* I'd sniffle *I lost my quarter. Could I please borrow a quarter from you? Oh honey,* pat pat on my head. *You don't need to pay me back. How cute. Here's some money for you dear child.* And I'd buy a box of Good & Plenty, small bullet shaped licorices coated in a thin layer of pink or white sugar. I'd suck the hard outer layer, sink my teeth into the saliva softened black flesh at the heart of it, feel the thrill of something for nothing, feel the thrill of outsmarting my mother.

Or I'd steal a dollar from my brother's wallet for the

next Nancy Drew in the series, steal a quarter and a penny from my mother's change purse for a pack of Kent cigarettes, smoke them out the bathroom window just as I did a few years later when I lit up a joint and got high.

Then cutting high school and the subway ride into the city with an empty suitcase before the days of electronic trackers. Records, clothes, jewelry, small appliances, anything that caught my eye, anything that fit in the suitcase. Shoplifting with Bonnie my best friend, shoes and sweaters and shit we threw away afterwards, old lady gloves and linen handkerchiefs, *why the hell did we steal this*? Laughing, doubled over on 5th and 54th, Top of the Sixes for lunch and *let's leave before the check arrives.*

I'd thought I'd be happy if only I had that outfit or that coat, so I'd slip it on and wear it out, hoping to be transformed into the beautiful slim girl my mother so desperately wanted, the one who got picked for teams, got the lead role in Oklahoma instead of the bit part of the flirt.

I thought with the right clothes I'd be the golden girl destined for greatness instead of the one facing an endless parade of guys with their dicks in their hands looking for a safe harbor. I'd be the fairy tale child raised in the castle, a nursemaid to bathe me, the king, my adoring daddy, to take me hunting, teach me how to bring down birds with a bow and arrow.

I'd be the virgin bride in the size 6 wedding dress. Something borrowed something blue. My aunties weeping silently into monogrammed hankies in the second row, the first row filled with mother father brother cousins all the beloveds here to celebrate my happy day, share my joy, sprinkle it like confetti on a shimmering future spread out beneath my feet.

Nancy London

# The History Dogs Are Barking

LISTEN. THE HISTORY DOGS are barking in the kennel. Tell it like this, they say, how your daddy died when you were twelve-years-old and your breasts were already formed. How you bled every month. How you refused to see him lying in his coffin because no, he could not possibly have died and left you with the Death Mother. But yes. He did.

The dogs are barking. Tell it like this. How you lost your virginity at fourteen to the lifeguard with the curly chest hair who was also a virgin and it was sweet and lasted a while. But ho hum. It doesn't really get to what I'm trying to find in the cellular memory of my skin.

Like this? How she made love with a heart heavy as a stone, the full moon looking in through the dirty window, a child with a man on top of her. His name? Who cares.

And the others? Of course there were others. Many others. But here's the thing: my body was not there, and without sensation there's no memory. So big reveal. I don't remember much of it, the too many men, the false ID, the long nights in the dark bars in Greenwich Village when I was 12, 13, 14, and 15. Grown men who looked at me like I was an all-you-can-eat shrimp buffet there for the gobbling. Okay. I was. Who cares.

So what do I remember? What was I present and accounted for?

Up in my second floor bedroom, dinner a Three Musketeers candy bar either stolen or bought with money I panhandled. There. A real memory.

True Confessions magazines. Naked women with breasts as big as mine, wet hot flooding between my legs. Yes. There. I was alive, rubbing until I shuddered. I was there.

And my small white radio, the early days of rock and roll, the DJ Alan Freed spinning Chuck Berry, Bill Haley and the Comets, Elvis, the Platters. More wet between my legs. More *yes* I'm alive.

And the Apollo Theater in Harlem where we waited, two white girls in a sea of brown and black, lining up at 1am for a 9pm show. *I'm sleeping at Bonnie's,* I'd say to my mother, who was too weary, too beaten down by grief and despair to look out for me anymore. Little Richard in a chartreuse satin suit, the Everly Brothers so sexy, so hip swively, I knew for those few hours I had found a place to lay down the stone in my heart and dance free in the aisles.

Do I remember coming home? Fighting about where I'd been, smelling of cigarettes and late night subway funk? No, I don't. Do I care? Sometimes. Sometimes I want the barking dogs to say: Here. Here's your life, goddammit. Don't you remember? And no, I don't.

Do I care? Yeah. I do.

*And the body said to the soul: where have you been?*
*And the soul falls down laughing, rolling in the grass, eating flowers and cuddling the moon.*
*Where have I been?* she laughs. *Where did you look?*

Nancy London

THE RIPENING | Seed

# Hunger

SHE'S SO BEAUTIFUL, they said to the mother. What a lucky mama to have such a beautiful baby.

But then baby grew up, grew confused and angry. Grew thorns. Grew fat.

You could be so beautiful if only you'd lose some weight, the aunties said.

She used to be so beautiful, they whispered behind her back. What happened?

Everyone felt so sad watching beauty sail out to sea.

I held on to her, tried to catch a ride. Tell me what to do, I begged. Don't leave me. No one will love me if I'm not beautiful.

Well, she said, there are a few rules. Are you willing?

Anything, I gasped.

First. You must never *ever* allow yourself to be hungry.

What?

Yes. If you're hungry you lose all your chips in this game. Chew gum. Smoke cigarettes. Don't even look at a steak or a ripe piece of fruit. Consider a carrot. Maybe celery.

But wait.....

No buts. Are you in?

Ok.

Next. Always have a mirror handy so you can check to see if there's any food caught between your teeth. That's ugly.

Ok. Check. Mirror. She gave me a small mirror that fit into the back pocket of my too-tight jeans.

She sat down, took my hand, gazed into my eyes. And finally. You must get rid of your fat. Fat is disgusting.

Yes, I agreed quickly, wiping the sweat off my face. Fat is disgusting.

Do we have a deal?

We do.

So beauty unpacked and we set up shop. She showed me how to measure portions and how to throw up after a meal.

But then the diseases. Adrenal fatigue. Tooth decay. Sorrows that had no name. And hungers that drove me out of bed at night to forage for real food, for the nourishment I'd need to keep me alive. Chicken. Asparagus. Lentils and butter. Sweet potatoes. Moroccan lamb stew. A hunger that screamed to be fed, then wept at beauty's feet when she threatened, cajoled.

Get up! Throw up! Don't give up!

Go away, I begged. Leave me in peace.

Beauty left her calling card on the fridge. She used to be beautiful, it said. I tore it into small pieces and ate it.

Gelato. Papayas. Mangoes.

You could stop eating, she called as she rowed out to sea.

Not a chance, I called back.

Coconuts. Bananas. Ripe figs.

Nancy London

# The Voice of the Wound

I was the girl decked out all in white with a flower tucked behind my ear, sitting at the feet of a guru. He gave me a new name, a secret name which roughly translated to *the voice of the mother.*

This was disturbing. My mother's voice was the last voice I'd want to hear coming out of my mouth, and I was not yet a mother myself. And as for the Divine Mother…she was way *way* out of my league. I simply could not conjure a benign maternal presence.

And then there were the astrologers who looked at my chart, at Chiron the wounded healer stuffed in with five other planets in Virgo into the third house of words and communication. *Hmm,* they'd say, tapping the pie slice of paper. *The voice of the wound.*

Fuck you, I'd think as I left. Who the fuck wants to be the voice of the wound? I wanted to be one of the shiny girls. You know…Sun Ra, Kali Rainbow, or Ananda Kiss My Ring and leave your love donations in the basket by the front door.

But I wasn't. I'm not.

So one night I was sitting out on the front porch under a star drenched sky when a FedEx truck rumbled down the gravel driveway. It seemed odd so late at night, but maybe it was an Amazon Prime thing.

Special delivery for you, honey.

He tossed a package over the adobe wall, whistling, keeping time with the wind in the willows. The return address in purple ink: From the voice of the wound.

Hey wait, I called. She doesn't live here anymore.

He leaned out his window and winked. That's what she said you'd say, and disappeared under the soft shushing of starlight falling to earth.

Open me, she said.

Drop dead, I said, and she laughed soft as a hummingbird.

Go on, there's a gift inside.

Yeah, that's what my uncle used to say before he unzipped his pants.

But it was easier than I thought to get inside, following the arrows pointing down and down and down.

Keep going, she said.

There was nothing inside but darkness. That's it? This is the gift? I scraped my chair back and began to get up.

Deeper, she said. *Deeper.*

And then I heard it.

The call of the coyote. The milky mewing of a newborn learning to suck. The sigh of the moon as she blooms and gives birth.

The songs of the whale the blackbird and starfish came pouring out, singing one vast high note of joy, of endless waves of love that conquer grief and loss and despair. It was the song of rainbows arcing over oceans and thunder in the desert. It was every victory song that has ever been chanted, banged, hooted, stomped and hallelujahed.

Here, she said, handing me a rose. Now sing this.

Nancy London

# Where I Found You

WHEN I CAME FOR YOU it was raining. I had to hack my way through the honeysuckle that had grown over the fence and pick my way over the cracked concrete. But still. I knew where to look for you.

I entered our childhood home by the front door, all the furniture still in place. The oil portrait of you and your big brother still hanging over the sofa. The silver tea set on the coffee table. I went up the stairs to your room because that's where you always were, listening to the radio, The Lone Ranger and later, rock and roll.

When I found you I knelt beside you and called your name, but you didn't answer. You were curled up under the heavy quilt with the tiny roses, and the wallpaper, dainty, pink and white flowers, the way a girl was supposed to look.

I lifted the blanket and wept. You were weightless, almost transparent. I could see your lungs and heart struggling to pump, the effort it took to breathe in and out.

Come with me, I said. I'll take care of you. But you did not stir.

Come honey, please. I reached out my hand but you lay limp, eyes empty and dull. You made a small sound and I bent to hear you.

Help, you said. Help.

I threw back the covers and raised you up under your arms, lifted you over my back the way firemen carry the rescued. You clung to my neck and we descended the stairs, past the portrait and the silver, past the bookcase, the upright piano, past the framed family photos and out into the light.

We rested on the grass next door. You lay in my lap, watching the wind in the trees, watching the storm only you could see brewing. And then it howled like all the dead and their sorrows, smashed the windows of our childhood home, blew down the doors. The wind rampaged through the house, every corner, every closet, until nothing remained of the past that had waited for me to make my way home to find you.

# Breast Stroking Home

My brother Jake comes back from the dead and peers over my shoulder.

I don't want no stinkin eulogy, he says.

Well too bad, I say, because that's what I'm writing about tonight, so leave if you want to.

He hesitates, shifts the toothpick to the other side of his mouth.

So what? he says. What are you going to write about me?

No worries, I say. It will all be the truth.

He flashes his half grin and I begin.

My brother. My brother was broken from the time he was a small child. I could not fix him although I tried. He was dark and beautiful, tall and thin, but later grew short and fat like a toad.

Hey, he yells. No fair.

It's true, I say. The anger turned you into a troll, like in a fairytale.

The best part about my brother, I continue, was his

wicked sense of humor. We cracked each other up. Really bad dark sick jokes that doubled us over. What's so funny? our mother would ask, and we'd look up, helpless. Nothing, we'd gasp. Really. Nothing.

Yeah, I remember, he says.

And another great thing about my brother, I go on. One summer when he was a swanning sleek teen he worked at Abe's deli and we stayed at our grandmother's summer home a block from the beach. Remember the pickled green tomatoes you'd bring me? I ask and we smile.

Yeah, he says. They were good.

My brother. He was, now don't try to stop me because it's true, he was always a bit crazy, like a sociopath, a criminal, a mafia kind of guy, a hustler who made millions in his father-in-law's silk flower business.

Well, Jake says now, there was a little something on the side you didn't know about.

But my brother, I say, my brother was the one my mother came to when she wanted to end her life.

Hey, he calls softly from the door. Don't go there, please. Please.

My brother, I continue, was happy to help her die, roped me into the whole fucking mess. And now I'm sweating and pacing, like maybe this isn't the sweetest eulogy all of a sudden.

And Jake says, please. I beg you. It's been a long time, twenty cow years if you're counting, and I'm doing my time in a place I can't tell you about, but it's hard work. It's fucking hard work. So if you have to carry on please just say...by the time he died, he died alone and was very crazy and very sad, but he's doing better now.

Which I guess is what I want to tell you. Even the broken find their way home.

There is a humpback whale named Moon. She has been swimming from British Columbia to Maui, making slow progress because her back was broken by a speed boat. She can only use her dorsal fins. She is breast stroking all the way home, losing weight, lice and algae attached to her wound. Swimming through the long days and nights to return to the place where she was born. She will die there from exhaustion, malnutrition, maybe from loneliness.

I check on her progress every morning. She's made it back to Maui.

This is an elegy for Moon who will die soon. Who knew how to find her way home.

Rest in peace, Moon.

Rest in peace, Jake.

And may the eternal flame of love light the path for all of us who are making our way home.

Nancy London

## Speak, Silence

My grandmother was not a great cook, but what she did know how to do was brew cherry wine from the enormous fruit tree in her backyard.

Her devoted neighbor Nick dragged the ladder out from the garage and harvested the abundant crop every summer, then helped her fill the crock pots in her basement where it simmered for at least six months. My Aunt Sylvia helped put up the hooch in quart jars and then distribute them to my grandmother's neighbors in time for the holidays, always an extra quart or two for Nick, who also shoveled the snow from her sidewalk, and to her seven grandchildren who elbowed each other out of the way to receive this holy communion.

Never once did she speak to us of her journey across the ocean, alone, in steerage, eating cold potatoes and throwing up in a bucket. Never once did she talk of her mama and papa, sisters and brothers shot by the Cossacks, or the village set on fire, or the babies, oh god the babies, killed with bayonets. I did not understand that all those years I was drinking her wine I was also swallowing her words.

My father moved through the house shadow thin, always getting ready to die, always dressed in clean underwear, as if that mattered if we found his corpse. He whistled, filling the air with the romantic tunes he made up, added to, left to trail him from room to room and out the front door without a backwards glance. I learned to whistle his broken melodies but never asked what silenced him, what drove his words so deep inside all he had left for me was bird language.

Aunts and uncles, cousins, my brother, my mother, my beloved friends and lovers, all gone, leaving me holding my tongue, always asking - is it safe to speak?

What will happen to me if I am loud?

What if I cry out in anguish or in pleasure?

What if my grief spills over the measured line or my laughter rouses the neighborhood dogs?

What if I speak up in a crowd?

What if I disagree or say *no*. Or say *I don't want to*. Or say *stop you're hurting me*. Or say *hey get your hands off me*. Or shout *help. Somebody help.*

What if I break the silence that broke the ones that came before me, weep for them, dance for them, touch the sky for them. What if I declare myself deserving of this life. Of safety. Of home. Of love and acceptance. What if I turn to them now and say, *you were silent but I heard you. You died choking on words but I heard them.*

What if I place my hands on my heart and say, *you are safe now. Speak.*

# Part Two

---

# WATER

Nancy London

# Knock Knock Joke

KNOCK KNOCK.
 Who's there?
 Boo.
 Boo who?
 Hey, don't cry, honey. It's not so bad. Really, everything will work out for the best. You'll see.
 Is she batshit crazy? I'm dying here, drowning in grief, weeping right in front of her and she's telling me it's not so bad?
 I'm sad, I'm sorrowing, I'm grieving.
 I miss my father, I finally say.
 Really? When did he die?
 Er....when I was twelve years old.
 Wait. You're telling me he died like a million years ago and that's why you're crying?
 Haven't you cried enough? Aren't you just a little bit ashamed of yourself, carrying grief around like a baby blanket, curled up in the corner boo-hooing? Get a grip,

darling. It's over. Buck up. Man up. Balls up. Grow up.

Get over it. Move on.

Just kidding, I want to say, fast, to swat away the heavy fog of shame that's settling over me.

Honestly, I say, I barely remember him. So how are you?

Listen. Here's the thing about grief. It does not go quietly into the land of the gray havens, retire, catch the next flight to a tropical island, open a beach chair, order mai tais and say *We have wept enough, gnashed our teeth, pulled our hair, fallen weak on the floor begging for relief, for death. Now, now it's over.*

I wish I could say that's how it goes. That one day grief will be gone, tied up with a blue satin ribbon like a bundle of old letters stored in a shoe box in the back of your closet, because Listen. One day a stranger wearing the perfume your mother wore will rip a hole straight through your heart. Or you'll see a man in the produce aisle of the grocery store who looks like your husband, dead five years, and the foundation will rock, the shelves will tilt, porcelain teacups will shatter, mirrors crack and that pack of letters? That neat pile of grief you tucked away will come tumbling down, spilling over your freshly swept floors, moaning the way something that has been kept too long in captivity moans.

There is nowhere to tuck sorrow where she doesn't start crying so loud you have to stop what you're doing and go investigate.

You left me in the closet, she weeps when you open the door. You don't love me.

Well, um, of course I do. I was just trying to get a few things done around the house.

You were trying to forget about me.

Well, not exactly. Sort of.

But when I finally take her in my arms and tuck a damp strand of hair behind her ear, wipe her tears with the hem of my tee shirt, I see that she's really quite lovely. Not at all the ugly child I was ashamed of. She has a peace and serenity about her I had not noticed before. Her presence quiets the rush of anxiety in me, the always in motion need to keep the floors swept, the dishes washed, the mirrors windexed.

She slows me down, and in the next deep breath that opens my lungs and the secret door to my heart, she slips in and smiles.

Mind if I stay here for a while? I promise I won't hurt you.

What can I say. I let her stay.

Sometimes when she needs my attention - the anniversary of my father's death, the babies lost to miscarriage, the year my daughter left home, I stop the endless busyness and sit with her, light candles, pick a bouquet of wildflowers, feed the crows.

And then I am still enough to feel the presence of the ancestors - the ones who carried their grief over mountains and across frozen rivers to reach me. The old ones who watched armies torch their homes and floods wash away all they had cultivated. The ancient ones who sent children to safety over oceans before the Cossacks arrived. Who hid in barns and in basements, who forged false papers, faced the rapist, the barrel of the gun, and said, my child - these stories need telling and retelling.

This is the story of our grief as we perished, they say. But it is also the story of the life we cherished.

Now, they say, open your heart and let the songs of mercy and forgiveness harmonize. Welcome the blackbird and the coyote who sit at your feet while you chant the holy names of life passed down on the lips of the peacekeepers. Let the music echo in the canyons so that yes and no weave together, the endless hum of always.

Your tears will fill the dry river beds and your weeping will shake the ripe fruit from the trees.

If grief did not stretch your heart to welcome your

own sorrow, how could you bear witness to the beautiful and terrible fellowship that comes with suffering?

How could you hold the news of floods and drought, of punishing winds and melting ice caps, if you could not extend mercy to your own earthquakes of despair and loss?

Blessed are the wounded for when our wounds cease to be a source of shame, we become wounded healers.

Where else but in the chambers of the broken hearted will we find the grace to dance with light and shadow.

Who else but the grieving are wise enough to crack open the sorrow and joy of the world and feast at the table of love.

Nancy London

# Rock and Roll

It's rock and roll, baby, that's where you'll find the grief. The young girl walking the streets of London with Procol Harum's *Whiter Shade of Pale* blasting from every café and vinyl record store. How can you not drop to your knees when you hear it now, rock back and forth, keening like the dying breath of the last whale, the cry of the trapped fox. How can you not look back upon yourself wandering those city streets, LSD from a hip new laboratory singing through your veins, your very life an origami the wind is softly unfolding.

It's rock and roll baby that will tear you open and pluck out your eyes, dancing all night under strobe lights with your tribe, high on mescaline and then wrapping up in shawls and blankets and waiting, waiting, waiting - how can you not hear *Here Comes the Sun* and not moan like the arrow of time and longing has just been lodged in your breast.

We were brave then without memory, the memory

we stashed at the back of the closet. *Later dude* we said. *We'll come back for you,* but of course we never did, because memory would have crippled us, and we needed our strength for the journey. We did not want to remember how we got the scars, why we still bled.

And oh my god to hear Leon Russell bang away on the piano and you are in that sweaty nightclub in Malibu and he's on that tiny stage so huge, so gargantuan, the piano like a ship he's sailing out into eternity. It's rock and roll, darlin'. How can you hear the opening chords from that massive man playing that massive piano and not stop up your ears, beg for mercy because, baby, it's the heartbeat of the reckless, the two-step of the abandoned, the waltz of the damned, the young ones who thought rock and roll was their flag, their anthem, the streetcar to ride them all the way home to the happy havens.

But we know better now, don't we? We hear *Tiny Dancer,* Elton pouring it out like hot sperm, like everything he's got coming at us all at once, singing wake up it's over didn't you know. We're here to break your hearts until you are begging for mercy, begging for a simpler time, a symphony, but please jesus not an opera because there's Verdi's *Otello* killing his Desdemona, singing, finally, the blind fool, of his mistake, his fatal mistake, and he takes us all down with him to the place where we can finally grieve for what we lost or killed by accident, with a word or a deed or a careless act of omission.

It takes us down to the cellar of our being where the wild beasts live, those who have no language, only the mournful sound of late night traffic in the rain, of wind chimes in a storm, of losses that sound one high note again and again and again, where we remember *Summertime*, the lullaby our mother sang to us, so sweet and soft, a coo, a promise, and we close our eyes and pray for daylight so that we might rise up off our knees and praise the world with a new sound, a new song. Where like the trees we throw caution to the wind and no longer need to be saved from love.

Nancy London

# Soft Candies and Hard Whiskey

WHEN I SAW THE SMALL AD for a hospice social worker I was zapped, the current straight from the hand of the merciful goddess into my broken heart. It was the year after my mother's suicide, and my intuition was screaming that only the dying could bring me out of the land of shadow, back into the light.

I sat across from the man tasked with interviewing me. Native American with a skinny dark braid, a Hawaiian shirt, and a slow easy smile.

So, he said, why do you want this job?

I was sweating. Under my arms. Between my legs, between my toes.

OK I said. This is no time for bullshit. My mother died bitter and sorrowing, cut off from love, and now I need to be in the same room with death again. Maybe a distant cousin to the death I just spent time with, or a step-kid. But I need to know there are other ways to die - better ways, holier, more sacred ways. Ways more filled with light and love.

He drummed his fingers on the metal desk. Any experience?

Nope.

He lined his pencils up so that all the points were shoulder to shoulder. Personally I would have gone with the erasers, but whatever.

I waited. I kept sweating. A small fan blew the papers around on the desk. I held my breath.

When can you start? he finally asked, and I exhaled.

And sweet jesus what a ride. Every time I knocked on a door, and stepped into the rooms of the dying, I entered with my heart beating like a little tin drum. I never knew who or what I'd find. Families in conflict or harmony, the dying in a state of acceptance or terror, siblings arguing or agreeing. I had begun the job with no training, and hadn't read even the most basic books on death and dying, but I was drawn like an iron filing into those rooms.

The doors opened and I walked into living rooms, bathrooms, tiny screened in porches, and the dying were there - in bed, in wheelchairs, on the pot, holding onto the kitchen counter while they struggled to make a cup of instant Nescafe.

They were toothless, hairless, limbless. They were finally without one small grain of hope. They were going to die. We both knew it, and it made everything hugely tragic and hugely funny. They told me bawdy jokes, the ones their chaste Catholic wives of 60 years had banned from the house. They scratched their balls or showed me their scars. They were so far gone into dementia that when they saw me, all they could say was *woohoo woohoo* and I'd say *woohoo* back and we both were so ecstatically happy with this exchange. I brought them the green chile cheese burgers they craved, then held back what little hair they had left as they heaved over a bowl.

Their every breath was labored, their legs no longer worked. Some were blind and mostly deaf. They spent a good percentage of their time in the land of the spirits. And still, I began to understand why it was worth it for them to live another day. The great grandbabies brought by for a visit, the nephews and nieces who sent flowers on Mother's Day. I saw a thread of love connecting people that was sturdier than it looked. The love that kept them here one more sunrise, one more cloudless sky. They knew they were dying, and they were filled with despair for things left undone, with regrets for what had been left unspoken.

They knew they were dying and they were filled with grace.

They burned from the inside, lit up with last minute

love, like a treasure you'd find at the bottom of a bargain bin. This was love that had nowhere to go except into the void, love that would never make love again, or eat a steak or run on a beach. Love that would die when they died, but for now, they burned with it and they let me love them back with everything I had. Everything my mother had refused.

They were the elders of our tribe, on fire with wisdom. And when it was time, I saw them open their arms to their long departed husbands, children, grandmothers, the beloveds who had come to walk them through the veil.

They brought me out of the land of death into the world of the living.

They taught me to kneel to the mystery of my life, to let grief dance with wild joy.

They taught me to ask for mercy and forgiveness from the earth, the trees, the animals before it was too late.

They showed me I could trust my most decent and compassionate impulses, and that I could find meaning in the calling of my heart.

They offered me kindness and generosity and told me how easy it could be to forgive myself. They asked me to try, for their sake.

Now that they have passed into the realm of the ancestors, I light candles for them on the solstice. I put out soft candies and hard whiskey, and from the far reaches of darkness they arrive with victory songs, beating drums and trailing clouds of glory, a radiant bunch of gypsies come to bring back the light.

Nancy London

## Magic Mushrooms

Before cell phones and social media, back in the day when an influencer was someone who knew where to get great weed and there was nothing but endless good day sunshine, I traveled with a boyfriend in an old white Ford van 10,000 feet up into the Oaxacan mountains in southern Mexico in search of *los hongos*, the magic psilocybin mushrooms.

It was a hot summer and I was busy being a radical feminist in Cambridge Massachusetts, writing pamphlets insisting the work women were doing inside the home - the endless 24/7 cycle of dishes cooking childcare cleaning and laundry was just as important and paycheck-worthy as their husband's work outside the home. True. But honestly, I was single and had miles to go before I understood anything about what binds two people together.

It was during that heady time that my friends began returning from the Oaxacan Mountains in southern

Mexico with fantastic stories of *los hongos*, the psilocybin mushrooms that grew wild there. My boyfriend Robbie asked if I'd be interested in buttoning up my life for a month and heading off to find them.

Yes. I would.

Did I have to think twice?

Nope.

This adventure called to me like a long forgotten wish, a genie let out of the bottle.

Robbie and I spent a sweaty July outfitting his Ford Econoline with a primitive double bed up on plywood, a cook stove and a basic pantry. Candles and incense, matches and lots of pot. We crossed the border at Nogales and kept heading south, driving endless miles along the Mexican coast, *Sweet Baby James* on the cassette player. We parked the van at night on empty beaches, ate papayas and guavas and fried fish we bought from local fishermen along the way.

We found X marks the spot on the pencil-drawn map outside the town of Oaxaca, climbed the mountain on a twisting one lane dirt road, pulling over into a turnout barely big enough to let a school bus pass, raising dust as it headed down the steep incline. We drove until we were inside the clouds. Up. Up. Up. Where was earth if we were so close to sky?

And then a plateau. We passed a small graveyard, an adobe store front, slowed, crawled, rolled to a halt in front of an ancient brown man waving, waving. He introduced himself. Primativo, *a su servicio*. He was at our service. We spoke a little Spanish. Did *los hongos* grow here? He bowed, smiled, then led us to a hut at the far end of the road. A plank bed, a thin mattress, a ceramic basin and pitcher, a towel. We were in the guest house. He gave us a warm stack of tortillas wrapped in a white cloth, lit the candle and retreated.

Each morning for the next three weeks Primativo waited for us just after dawn and guided us into the cow pastures to gather dozens of mushrooms off fresh cow patties. He showed us which ones to eat, *los hongos*, the magic ones, and which ones to avoid.

Fog hugged us, whispered low incantations, parted long enough to show us the next and the next and the next mushroom, and when I looked down from that height, the clouds were a pillowy bed far below.

We ate mushrooms every morning, and then ate the lunch Primativo would bring - simple vegetable soups, more tortillas, endless tortillas, fresh cheese. And always more mushrooms. We drank clear cool well water. The world was lit up, animate. Rocks mumbled, wild greens gossiped. The wind sang lullabies. The stars winked, laughed out loud.

Primativo put a galvanized tub under our bed filled with dark rich soil and then added spores, saying they would grow more mushrooms should we desire to eat any after dark. We did. We grew light headed, light footed. We grinned our heads off with his wife and daughters who came to inspect the whiteface strangers. Shy, giggling, they offered sweet cakes and dark tea brewed from fresh herbs.

Time grew slippery. I remembered and then didn't remember who I was and then didn't care. I was vibrating to the song of the earth and stars, greeting the low mosses that whispered my name as I walked among them. Energy collected on my hands and I blessed all I touched and was blessed in return. *Los hongos* pulsed with electricity. I swallowed sparks and lit up like a cathedral. Time moved sideways and backwards, time stood still, and then time lurched forward and it was time to go.

We said goodbye to Primativo, to his family, to the nameless children aunts and uncles who had looked after us from a distance. When I stood for one last time on the cliff at the top of the world, the sky opened and a soft voice filled my head.

It's time to seek a teacher of pure love.

Love?

Love.

I said yes, reached my arms out to the world above and below, said yes because I yearned for pure love. Hadn't I been seeking it with the full force of my desire, chasing it down dead ends and dark alleys, mistaking it for sex but all the while hadn't I been Diana the Huntress pursuing her prey? Of course I said yes.

I craved the ultimate lover who would know my innermost desires, who'd understand the tenderness I needed, who would match me passion for passion, the one who would turn me to liquid fire, our chakras pressed together exploding in ecstasy from orgasm up to the highest union with the Divine.

I craved a god lover, one who would whistle for me through the back door, ask what I was doing tonight, then flag down a cab and take me into the city to hear live music, drink vodka, dance until dawn. A god lover who would take me home, anoint my body with oil and then come into me as creativity, unity, the naughty and nice of it that would leave my legs shaking.

Of course I said yes. I said yes, and yes again, then wrapped up in a cloud, stepped off the cliff and into the arms of Fate.

I left Robbie playing Dylan covers in People's Park, found a ride on a bulletin board going straight through from Berkeley to Cambridge, and for the next 3,000 miles, with stops only for bathroom breaks and greasy take-out, I shared the backseat with Mrs. Gorilla, a slobbering pregnant brown and white springer spaniel.

I sold everything - my car, my stereo, my skis, my fancy clothes and four inch heels. It seemed impossible that I had been wearing these suits and blouses only a month ago. I barely recognized myself in the mirror. Who was this woman leaving everything behind, moving to California, searching for a teacher of love?

# Mermaid

He was tacked up on a wall inside the local hardware store the first time I saw him. I had a few minutes to wait while my compost was being loaded onto the back of my pickup, so I wandered over to the poster behind the rifles and stared. He stared back. The lean face with the ink black eyes, long flowing dark hair pushed high off his forehead. A black and white mandala behind him that appeared to vibrate. He was beckoning the spiritually hungry, the soul starved, the seekers of pure love, inviting us to attend a free seven lecture series on the chakras, starting Friday in Triple Creek, two towns up the narrow mountain road.

"Finally," I said out loud. "There you are." I had been looking for him, or someone like him, all during the autumn, attending one and then another disappointing spiritual talk by some immature blowhard with delusions of grandeur. My boyfriend Robbie thought the message to search for a teacher of pure love was a hallucination, something I had conjured to romanticize our time in Oaxaca, so I drove up to Triple Creek alone.

At 7pm sharp, the guru swanned into the room and folded his long legs in one graceful motion onto a white silk cushion. Wearing a red silk Nehru shirt, his eyes burned like a match through paper. He began strumming his guitar, chanting Om, vibrating the air, forcing the molecules to jump and sizzle. Everyone had their eyes closed but not me. I sat in the front row, focused on this man who might be the teacher of pure love the magic mushrooms had directed me to find.

He cleared his throat and began talking about the red chakra, the base, the bottom line where sexuality and life force are awakened. On and on about how to channel it, use it for creativity, send it up the spinal column for higher purposes. When the lecture was over, the guru's wife Wendy, who looked to be a million years older than him, everything about her sad, sagging, defeated, worn out like the cardigan draped over her thin shoulders, announced tea and cookies and we all filed into the kitchen to help ourselves. The guru stayed seated on his cushion, receiving people who bowed, thanking him for such a profound experience. I was barely able to glance in his direction because I was lit like a neon flashing sign semaphoring awakened red level energy.

Six more Friday nights up through the chakras. Orange chakra with an orange silk shirt, yellow green blue indigo violet all with matching silk shirts and appropriate lectures on the spiritual meaning of each energy center. I'd come home from Triple Creek feeling spiritually exalted and walk into a web of cigarette and pot smoke, Robbie and a few of his friends getting high and playing blues guitar. One night I exploded, began throwing empty beer bottles at Robbie, telling his friends to get the fuck out of the house. In retaliation, he disappeared for two days.

We hadn't planned on it, but I was three months pregnant and carrying twins. I had already miscarried twice, the last one a small fetus I had flushed down the toilet, pregnant only six weeks. Despite the growing differences between us, I wanted to keep the baby. When the phone rang on the second day of his disappearance, I stood quickly to answer it. It was a wrong number, but before I could hang up, blood gushed out of me thick, hot, red. It covered my feet up to my ankles.

I stuffed three towels between my legs, and stumbled into the back seat of a cab. The emergency crew came for me with a stretcher and skated me down the too bright hospital corridor. Every muscle was clenched, holding on to my babies for one last moment. They shot me up with something to relax me and dull the pain and in a blur of white coats and sharp instruments, I held on to a nurse's freckled arm while they scraped me out.

When Robbie returned home, he found the blood soaked kitchen floor, and tracked me to the small hospital recovery room. He started banging on the hospital rails in frustration, a rhythmic drum solo. He needed to drive south that night to his massive greenhouse and water his million dollar marijuana cash crop and couldn't wait around for me to be discharged. I was still bleeding, coiled over my womb. "Go," I said, wanting only for him to stop shaking the bed. "Go and don't come back."

For the next three months, a steady stream of friends showed up at my door bringing chopped liver, halvah, beets, raisins, anything they could think of to build my blood. They held me while I cried. My relationship was over, and for all I knew, the end of my chances to have a baby. I was flabby and had to crawl to the bathroom because I had lost most of the blood needed to keep me upright. The corner grocery store delivered toilet paper and toothpaste. I didn't have a TV, never saw a newspaper. There was nothing tethering me to earth.

When I could stand up straight without colliding into a wall and walk without having a dizzy spell, I made an appointment with the guru to discuss how I might become a member of the group forming around him. Wendy kept the calendar and booked me for the following Tuesday at noon.

We met in his backyard. His long body was draped in a lounge chair, and he was wearing what I would come to know as his standard uniform - pressed trousers and a starched white shirt. Cufflinks. He was absorbed, writing on a yellow legal pad in long hand and finished a thought before he looked up. I approached timidly with no rehearsed words. I knew the heat I gave off would say everything, and that if our eyes met, desire mixed with spiritual longing would leap out panting like a Doberman on a short chain.

He nodded and indicated that I was to sit on the grass since he was in the only chair. OK I thought. Here I am at your holy lotus feet.

He took a sip of his beer and a bite of the sandwich I assumed Wendy had prepared for him. "So," he began, taking in the all of me, "why do you want to be my student?"

A flood of words. Oaxaca. The mushrooms. Seeking a teacher of pure love. His poster.

Oh holy fates how you must have twisted in the wind as you watched him assess me, watched me finally dare to tumble deep into the dark pools of his eyes until he reached in and dragged me back to the surface, nodding as I flailed on the shore, catching my breath.

"You are a bhakti," he said. "Someone who is destined to find God through the path of love. I believe you have come to the right place." He stroked my palm, smiling like we shared the secrets of the universe.

I was electrified. The rush of energy in my chakras must be the sign that I had finally found the teacher I needed to fulfill my promise to *los hongos*.

"You're a seeker," he said, wonder blooming in his eyes, a fisherman who has landed a mermaid.

I nodded. I am. I am a bhakti. I am a seeker of pure love. I am a young girl who misses her long dead father.

# Hands On

Shortly after my official entry into group life, I offered the guru a shiatsu massage on a Friday afternoon before his weekly Friday night public lecture.

I set my mat up in his living room, closed the curtain separating it from the kitchen, and waited. He blew in, six foot three, wearing white jockey underwear. My guru. My holy teacher. He flopped down on his back, his dark hair fanned out around him like a peacock. "Do me," he said.

Part aroused, part terrified, I worked on every part of his body. When I completed the circuit ending with him once again on his back, I was dazed, spinning dizzy from the love and devotion I had poured into him for 90 minutes.. He rose, ruffled my hair, then disappeared behind the curtain that had delivered him to me.

I heard from Wendy that the guru was pleased, and would like to continue the massages on a regular basis. Each Friday I arrived ten minutes early, set up my mat and waited. He'd arrive smelling of sandalwood, and open himself to me as I channeled the full force of my spiritual longing through my hands into his body. I nuzzled his hair as I worked on his scalp. Cautious, never going beyond the point that could be taken the wrong way. Cautious.

And then one Friday when the massage was over he made no move to get up, a glittering object waiting to be claimed. He ran his hand up my bare thigh, a silent invitation. This was what I had been seeking. Daddy. God. Guru. A blooming lotus from the tight core within me exploded out to the limits of the room and beyond where peace and light and the promise of spiritual and sexual love finally united.

He said, Give it to me. I can take all your love. And my old self kissed the young boys goodbye and came to him open and shimmering. Willing. Hungry. Ready to split myself open on the altar of love.

We made eye contact, one brief moment, and in that instant I saw my lover, my brand new lover who had just opened the gates of heaven slip away, vanish on the outbreath, and in his place, the guru, the one on whom I would learn I could make no claim. He was a love letter written in sand.

I sat in the front row during that evening's Friday

night public lecture, lit up like Chanukah and Kwanzaa and the Elks Club parade. I was plugged into a socket... the guru, spirit and me, sure he would at least glance my way, a twinkle, a wink or a nod, but he never looked, never stepped out of character - the Great Man, the wise one, the anointed holy one. The one above all human desire.

(And the therapist I was paying too much money to would cross his bony fingers over his starched white shirt trying to sound like fucking Freud and say: *So. Do you think this behavior has anything to do with looking for your father?*

*Of course it does, you moron.*)

Nancy London

# Hot Seat

THERE WAS A FEELING among the group that we were on the cutting edge of a revolution in consciousness. We had survived sex drugs and rock and roll, spit out at the end of that long siege, out of our senses, half out of our minds onto a windswept beach with no moral compass to steer by.

We arrived at the feet of the guru who promised a life filled with purpose, with service to a shattered world. Us. A small band of rag tag stragglers. He said he had created the tool for this cultural transformation and called it Nonviolent Conflict Resolution, NCR. We were all sick of conflict. Most of us had come from homes where conflict resolution meant someone stormed out of the room, slamming the door for emphasis. Or withdrew into an arctic punishing silence. Or used a belt or a switch or a fist and called the conflict resolved. Hadn't we had enough of trying to explain ourselves and skittering off the tarmac into the guardrail? Weren't we sick of living half-truths and whole lies?

We filed into his living room for our first session, carrying our cups of tea, our meditation cushions, excited, frightened, right on the edge. The guru led us in a brief meditation, and then asked who had a conflict that needed resolving.

It became a free for all. We were in uncharted waters and did not know how to rescue the drowning. This is what we later called a "bashing," people taking turns telling each other what they didn't like about them, careful to use phrases like "your ego" because the whole idea was to slay the ego so that we might attain the highest state of pure consciousness, The Absolute.

What the hell was The Absolute ? I don't think any of us had a clue. It sounded like a shiny prize we would never have enough green stamps pasted into our booklet to claim.

What I wanted was to steer clear of the "hot seat," another apt label generated over time. I did not want conflict, violent or nonviolent. I cared much more about being alone with the guru than I did about attaining The Absolute.

Mostly I hovered above the gutter sniping. I slid beneath the radar, sat quietly on my cushion, offered very little in terms of ego bashing. I liked these people. They were simple minded, a lot of them, but big of heart, and any fool could see they were devoted down to their last mala bead to the guru who took his own turn ego bashing for the sake of our purification, our evolution, for the sake of the greater good of the planet.

But sometimes it felt mean, spiteful, a discharge of venom; he'd rant about how he had given up on us, how we had disappointed him. Hadn't most of us disappointed our parents? Wasn't this more than we could bear? Didn't he know that? Didn't he care? The meetings turned brutal quickly, one after another of us berated by him, bashed, shamed, left cowering on our hard round cushions, the despair of having displeased the guru cutting so deep you could smell the blood.

Nancy London

## Mantra on Repeat

MY HEART FELT LIKE a coke can crushed under a boot as I watched Wendy caring for the guru. She did his laundry, shopped for the freshest produce, the most sublime cut of salmon hand-picked to keep his uber brain in tip top form. She washed and rinsed the lettuce, sliced radishes and carrots for the salad, put a pot of rice on to cook, all the while I stood behind his chair at the kitchen table and rubbed his shoulders across his ironed white shirt, down his spine, kneading, pressing, working out the kinks. While she was cooking I was sending wave after wave of Shakti energy into his body and he was receiving it and sending it back. We were electrifying each other. While she was cooking. The Great Man needed his massage and I was loosener of fascia, she who made nirvana bliss juice to flow.

I felt protective towards her. Even as I was betraying her. When I entered their kitchen he'd fondle my breasts in front of her. In front of her! Just a quick squeeze, something a playful man of God would surely do. But she'd wince and turn away, her shoulders caved in. She'd shrink from her willowy 5'8" down to an old woman, small, defeated.

I wanted to say *Don't do that* but no one challenged him, because opposition would of course require extensive correction in an endless violent nonviolent creative resolution session well into the night. Instead, I tried to duck before he could reach me, but he was too fast and she was too slow and there we were again, mother, father and me.

It became my obsessive mantra…how could he treat his wife like that? How could he treat his wife like that? Was he the real deal, a holy teacher of pure love or was he the biggest bullshitter abuser head tripper I had ever met? And if the latter, why the fuck had the mushrooms led me to him?

# The Hour of the Black Dog

RAIN RUNNING DOWN my bedroom window, the ratatattat of hail. Hail Mary, full of disgrace.

"I want a baby," I said. He was putting his clothes back on while I stayed tucked under the covers, massaging my empty womb.

"Children will sap your spiritual energy," he said. "You won't get far on the spiritual path thinking like that." He had done his disappearing act, my lover now gone and in his place the Great Man dispensing wisdom. I watched him put in his cufflinks.

"How can I want something so badly, and have it be wrong for me?" I was reading books about the nature of desire, how trusting one's deepest yearning was a path to ultimate spiritual fulfillment. It sounded truer than anything I had heard from him in a while.

"Desire is an illusion. Focus your attention on purifying your love." He was leaning down to tie his shoes and I admired the curve of him, the long line of spine like a whole fish skeleton on a platter.

"But I would love a baby with pure love," I countered. Insistent. Desire was a subject where I could hold my ground.

"That's not the same. Don't confuse worldly love with the highest spiritual love you are capable of." He meant loving him. Devoting myself to him.

My breasts leaked something viscous that stained my shirts. Maybe I had cancer. I had this mystery liquid analyzed by a lab. It turned out to be milk. They sent me the results with a handwritten note....we think you want to have a child. Well, yeah.

Desire sat up and got dressed. Washed between her legs, rinsed out her mouth, poured some vodka.

Did I hear you right? she asked him. You want to give this girl the world without a moon, the earth without water? You offer food but no salt, weather but no rain, home but no child?

Listen, she said. I know lots of people pay lots of money to hear you talk but honey, you just aint smart. There's only one thing you can offer this girl that will make her stay and that's a child. Do we have a deal?

We did not have a deal.

I got up and put on the white silk kimono he had brought back from a business trip to Japan. I walked him to the door. The rain blew in at a slant and I stepped back to watch him hurry to the Lincoln, glance around, check to see if anyone from the group had followed him. The rumor of our affair swirled through the substrata of our daily close - quarter group lives like a carnival shell game, slipping in and out of doors, disappearing from one role into another, wearing masks of aloofness and then switching to intimacy. Smoke and fun house mirrors. Isolation and self-deception.

He came to visit me during the hours of the black dog, 2 or 3am, when desire lawlessly roamed the streets and we would make love with the curtains drawn. He installed a red phone in my bedroom with a private number only he possessed. I was to answer it when it rang no matter the time. He'd call late at night when his wife was asleep and we'd talk about our love, how strange it was, how dangerous.

His Friday night lectures on the nature of pure love grew in popularity; he rented a meeting hall to accommodate the standing room only crowds. His books on the evolution of consciousness became New Age essential reading. The ever-expanding group that gathered around him began to treat him like the god he hinted he was. All of this worship of a man who continued to shatter his wife's heart and humiliate his disciples. His Friday night talks were aimed at me, lecturing on how a spiritual seeker risks losing the accrued merits of a hundred incarnations when worldly desire for a family arises. He hinted that I would come back as a cockroach in my next life if I defied him. Everything sounded like a crazy, grasping desperate attempt to terrify and control me; later at night, alone in the dark, my body shook with panic, unable to sort the grains of rice, afraid it might be true.

# Love Not Love

Sometimes, to clear my head I'd drive down the coast to Big Sur, sneak into Esalen and soak in their hot tubs under the stars. I'd sleep in my pickup by the side of the road, and when I'd get home he'd demand to know where I had been. Had I gone there for sex? Did I pick someone up in the hot tubs, someone who had been watching my titties bob in the hot water? Did I fuck someone in my truck? And then he'd forbid me to go to Esalen or to ever sleep in my truck again.

The more I rebelled, the more desperate he became. When I came home elated at 2am after drinking and dancing at the Catalyst, listening to a live performance by Tim Hardin singing If I Were a Carpenter, he was waiting for me outside my home, huddled in the Lincoln, hissing, begging, crying for me to behave.

His books and public lectures were all pinning him to the spiritual pop star map, but loving me was unhinging him. He drove with impatient accelerations and braking. His moods grew dark and he became irrational, threatening, driven to careless indiscretions and torrents of rage.

The red phone would ring, waking me from sleep. "What were you doing with Ted in the meeting tonight? I saw you put your hand on his knee."

"Don't be ridiculous. I'm not attracted to Ted in the slightest. I'd never put my hand on his knee." I struggled to sit up, to clear my head, to mass my soldiers along the border of my defenses.

"You're lying to me." He would hang up abruptly, leave me holding the red phone with a loud dial tone and a bedside clock blinking 3:36. The next morning he'd ignore me when our paths crossed, and I'd have to schedule a private meeting with The Great One to see if we could work some of this shit out. He'd be in High Guru mode, my lover disappeared, in place another weird thing I was supposed to do to win his favor back. He forbade me to drink coffee or shop for new clothes, and stop all ice cream consumption. It didn't matter. It was always something new, the equivalent of crawling on my knees begging for forgiveness.

Jealous, possessive, often over the edge with suspicion, I'd look out the kitchen window and see him spying on me, so I began eating all my meals in the bathroom with only one high window. Sometimes I'd hear the gravel crunch at night when I was in bed. A high beam would shine through the window, sweep over the blankets, the pillows, the corners of the room, scanning to make sure I was alone.

I wasn't sure he was even a decent human being, let alone God incarnate, but I had turned all my power over to him and now I wanted it back. Skin remembers the way a lover you thought was kind grips your arm and leaves a mark. Skin remembers so that when he approaches again with flowers, skin whimpers, contracts, shrivels up inside itself.

I was buried up to my eyeballs in the myth of the holy man with nothing but a plastic shovel to do the digging out.

Sweating, unable to sleep, I ate nothing but fudgsicles because I threw everything else up. He denounced me as a dangerous woman, set out rules for my punishment and made proclamations like the kings of old. No one was allowed to talk to me for 90 days, which meant I would move like a ghost in and out of morning meditation and evening Nonviolent Conflict Resolution meetings. Sweeping his long hair back over his shoulders, he declared I was to use this opportunity to repent repent repent and finally see him for who he really was.

He was a holy man to his students as he had once been to me, and they didn't take kindly to my acts of defiance. Night after night I was the center of NCR sessions. They kept me up for hours speaking in hushed voices - I was in tremendous spiritual danger, at risk of committing the ultimate crime of spitting on the pure love of the guru.

But was his love pure? I would get home from group meetings exhausted and confused, unable to trust my most basic instincts. Up at 5am for group meditation fortified with Earl Gray tea laced with a heavy dose of brandy, more NCR in the evenings until the hours and days blurred and my nerves were frayed hot wires one spark away from ignition. I was beginning to wonder if the mushrooms had misdirected me to see if I could find my way out of this maze of love/not love.

# Wild Strawberries

WHAT I NOTICED ABOUT RICHARD during those endless nights of NCR sessions was that he was thoughtful, refusing to bash anyone with the new age good-for-your-ego jargon that often ripped the heart out of a vulnerable member. He'd call me at 3am after a session to offer comfort. He had been reading the distress on my face, the mask everyone else mistook for composure. On the nights when the guru was out of town, he'd come over and bring two ceramic mugs of coffee and corn bread hot from the oven.

After months of damp clothes and mold in the shower, I watched winter melt and the crocuses elbow their way up and out from beneath frozen ground, naughty girls who mocked the white witch of winter in their frilly green dresses. Some days when the weather was nice we snuck away and stretched out on blankets along the river. I relaxed when we were together, fell into his brown eyes and easy laugh, took his hand when we walked because the heat he gave off warmed an exiled place inside me. Stray dogs came and flopped over, shamelessly exposing their bellies, begging, drooling. "Born in the Chinese Year of the Dog." His smile was blinding. "I don't know how else to explain it. They think I'm a relative."

*Hey. I want to lie on my back and have this big man with the big warm hands rub the ache in my belly.*

I cried when I told him about my miscarriages, how my insides still felt raw. He held me and I felt safe, like I had come home to reclaim a part of myself I had left on a cold sidewalk back in my childhood. This was uncharted territory – a non-sexual male friendship.

He was divorced, sharing custody of his twelve-year-old daughter Skylar with his ex. He talked about his Mormon childhood, the holy terror damnation hammered into him for simply being a child, all the fun he never got to have, how he had to watch TV through a neighbor's window on their front porch since his father thought that money, blacks, Jews and television were the roots of all evil.

His biceps were pure Michelangelo, sculpted from the years of summer labor baling hay for a neighbor. He blushed, claimed his physical strength was inherited from his Uncle Louie who had been the strong man in

THE RIPENING | Water

the circus. But despite his obvious alpha maleness, he never intimidated, and when we came to a four-way stop sign, he'd wait patiently for his turn, waving everyone else through first, while my foot tapped impatiently, aching to hit the accelerator while they all dithered.

I wondered what it would be like to live with him, if I could adapt, slow down. I wondered if I could cast off all the personalities and survival strategies I had perfected in order to secure love.

I wondered what our kids would look like - his smile, my green eyes.

I wondered if I could love a partner my own age instead of a stand-in daddy.

He was never too far away, willing to walk with me for hours through dark empty streets when anxiety became too much for my body to contain. He came courting with the love poems he wrote that spoke of marriage as the path to the divine. He offered me a vision of a holy radiant union we could call down from the heavens and claim as our own.

I wandered and thought. Tried to listen to my feelings as I rambled through the golden light that fell softly in the redwood forest. Occasionally Richard would meet me on a prearranged trail and we'd hike while I gathered medicinal herbs.

We could leave together, he said one day. I was holding a bouquet of chickweed, dock, young dandelion greens, wild strawberries the size of an infant's fingernail.

Leave together?

He confessed his love, proposed marriage, said he wanted more than anything to give me the child I yearned for. A rush of heat, a throbbing in my womb. He was offering me my heart's deepest desire.

I'm not ready, I told him, which was different than saying no.

# What Courage Said

Without offering any excuses, I skipped Friday shiatsu, skipped the Friday night lecture, and walked alone through the dark mostly empty town of Triple Creek. I stopped at Roz's office, the local masseuse. Her Open sign was in the window and her lights were on. It was a good place to hide out.

Inside was a man I hadn't met before. I thought maybe he was a monk, bald head, clear blue eyes, an air of peace and stillness he wore like a tunic. He welcomed me in and we exchanged small talk for a moment but I was obviously agitated, distraught.

"There's something on your mind," he said gently, and I began sobbing. "I need to be touched."

He led me to his massage table and for the next three hours cradled me as I gasped, cried and shook with grief and sorrow. I was a twelve-year-old child again and my father had just died.

Sweating and shaking, every cell in my body remembering my desolation, alone in my room eating stolen candy, finding a reprieve, a spark of life, in sex with older men, daddy everywhere and nowhere. I trembled remembering the love I lost long ago. I trembled with the terror that leaving the guru would carve out my insides and leave me as hollow and desperate as I had been without my father, abandoned to a living hell.

When the massage was finally over, the time of mourning my brokenhearted girlhood had passed. I had puked up enough of the old fears about the guru to trust myself. If I were to claim the love my heart longed for, the one thing I was certain of was that it would take a radical intervention to get clear of him.

Richard and I agreed to meet at a motel in Morro Bay, a three hour drive south. I would attend the next Friday night public lecture where the subject would inevitably be what damnation awaits a devotee who spits on pure love, then leave quietly and head down the coast.

But the guru was waiting by my car.

Where are you going?

Out. Down the coast. Anywhere. It didn't matter. Away from him was all that mattered.

You can't.

I can.

Don't you know who I am?

Only too well.

How dare you, he bellowed.

I dare, I bellowed back and kicked up gravel as I sped away.

It was a long drive. I had the windows down with the radio blasting rock and roll but I was tired and my nerves were jangled. I fell asleep at the wheel, woke suddenly, and pulled over.

Well you've done it now, Courage said from the back seat. No turning back. Are you scared?

I don't think so, I said.

How do you feel?

Like bees that have just found the orange blossoms. Like the silence of the first snowfall. Like my heart is unfolding its wings.

Are you happy?

Not yet, I said. I did what I had to do.

And would you do it again?

I think so, I said, sitting in limbo between one life and the next. I think I'd do it again. Maybe again and again. Maybe there's no way to know except to continue down the road.

Nancy London

# LSD With Buddha

I FLY INTO FORT MYERS, rent a car and drive across the bridge to Sanibel Island with two doses of LSD, fresh from a lab in San Francisco. A dealer friend has scored these for me, warning that the drug is strong. He recommends I pack at least two dozen apples. If I start spinning out of control, if sensations are flooding my body faster than I can handle them, bite into an apple. It will ground and steady me.

I check into a small motel perched at the end of the island, two steps out my door to a small private beach. It is May, the full moon, Buddha's birthday.

I unpack my apples into a plastic bowl, hang up my clothes, put on a bathing suit and plunge into the sea. The hallelujah sun is disappearing, melting like an orange popsicle, and the full moon is rising.

Buddha, I whisper. Happy Birthday.

Full Moon. Here I am. I have come to ask for blessings and guidance. I need help. Richard holds out his hand saying marry me and baby makes three. The guru says if I leave him I will be damned for spitting on pure love. Will I be damned for following the desires of my heart? Please. Come and guide me tomorrow as I open myself wide. Thank you.

I wake early, swallow one of the LSD doses with motel coffee, go out into the pale morning sun, slip into a tranquil sea. I swim until my muscles loosen from the long plane ride, then rest on the sand and let the salt dry on my skin. Just a few shell collectors hunched over, crab - walking along the beach, a small child throwing a Frisbee with her father. A yellow lab chasing skittering birds. More swimming, more resting, more waiting for the dose to kick in.

Nothing much is happening so I violate the first rule of psychedelics which is to *wait one hour* before dosing again, and so back in my room I take the second dose with another swig of motel coffee.

Back to the beach. More swimming. And then the world breaks up like a kaleidoscope, the sky and sea shifting, changing places, the sand undulating, the two-headed dog. I enter the sea, but there is no up or down and I give in, letting myself be swallowed by the whale. I open my mouth and laugh and then choke and know with sudden clarity that if I don't swim hard I'll die and I don't want to die and then I am stroking hard against a set of waves and then up on the shore finding my legs my towel my feet my flip flops. I shield my eyes Lawrence of Arabia across the Sahara to my door, the door that opens to let me slide inside the cool dark that holds me while I bite into an apple. Too late baby, way way too late. You've overdosed.

I take stock. I am grubby and need a shower but otherwise intact. Whoa. Slow to the shower. Hot water. The walls the ceiling the windows pulse. I careen across the room for my water bottle and the bowl of apples and collapse onto a nest of pillows and blankets

The room darkens and I am in a movie theater. A giant split screen flashes up on the bare wall. The spotlight shines: Screen One with the words SAFE PLACE in large glittering rainbow letters overhead. Richard is here. There's a gypsy wagon. He's moving about in the desert filling it with provisions. Pots and pans. Blankets. A cradle.

Screen Two: POWER in block letters. I am in an underground initiation chamber, a laboratory. The guru and I are working with light energies, moving mountains, experimenting with crystals. He is dazzling, while I am a novice in this world of subtle forces. He says he can teach me about pure love, and I worship him.

Screen One: Richard arrives at my tent. There are

heavy tapestries on the walls and floor. It is cool inside, and the light is clean, uncomplicated. He unpacks the provisions, brings the cradle and sets it at my feet.

Screen Two: I am a belly dancer in a harem. The favorite concubine. I hold enormous sexual sway over the Sultan. Scenes flash by in quick succession: I am a gypsy, a holy priestess doing a slow strip tease, a beggar, a queen, street hooker and slut. Mary Magdalene. And always it is the guru who is the god lover I am seeking.

I wear sandalwood on my pulse points, between my breasts. I wear a smile and lick my lips, sidle up to the guru lifetime after lifetime, grin and say pleased to meet you.

I wear a small knife and fork around a chain so I can consume him.

I wear desire like a neon flashing light, like starlight from Venus, like a car alarm that will not shut the fuck up.

I wear a sign that says, You. Only you.

I wear secrecy like a scent. Wrap up in fog and step through the night, find the back door enter slowly, avoid the third stair that groans, move like dust like baby hair through the house to the room where we meet.

I wear the smell of that room for days, the feel of the tile against my back, the cold wet grout marks like lashes. I am lashed by love.

I wear stealth like a pocket watch. I wear time like an enemy tick tocking away until I turn back into my solitude.

I wear my loneliness like a rash that breaks out in the heat, in the cold, when the wind blows and the branches beat their syncopation at my window.

I wear my solitude like punishment.

I wear the crime of needing too much on a wanted poster hanging on the wall.

I wear these lifetimes like a sack filled with feathers and rocks that I carry until my arms grow weary, my soul grows weary, my heart bursts like a child's balloon spilling out my hunger onto a rain soaked street.

I wear grief on my ragged sleeve like an honor, a medal from the merciful gods who take pity on the girl who wanted only love.

But I am too undone by my needs, by my insecurities. Too destroyed over having pursued love and found only power. Over time and through lifetimes my beauty fades. I become a hag dreaming in brown. I clutch and threaten. I commit a slow suicide with the poison plants that are my allies.

Lights up. I am gasping, sweating, my pulse is pounding. I take a few tentative steps, open my door and breathe breathe breathe the salt air, watch seagulls dive, listen to the laughter of children, waves scrubbing stone. Here. Now. I bite into several apples, leave them where they fall. Lights dim.

Screen One: I am in the mountains again. Oaxaca, standing at the edge of the cliff, open to the sky and the endless valley below.

You walked through fire, a voice says and it is the same voice I heard all those years ago, a young girl willing to risk it all to find pure love.

I did, I reply.

And then I am falling falling over the edge tumbling sailing caught by the breeze my dress a billowing parachute down through the clouds.

Richard and I are dressed in flowing white garments inside the shelter of our tent. There is no striving for a state I cannot attain, no reaching for a spiritual absolute that is not already contained in the peace and comfort that flows easily between us. There is a small sound from the cradle. I peel back the soft white blanket and look into the wide blue eyes of my laughing daughter.

A cloaked figure steps forward. She looks directly at me as if she were in the room. Maybe she is. I am pinned down like a butterfly. It is safe now, she says, to follow your desire. And here I slide off the bed because she throws off her cloak so I can see her red beating heart.

Lights up. I bite into an apple. I do not know how long I have been traveling through the realms of love and power, how many times I did or did not have to pee, how often I cried or laughed or gasped or held my breasts that leaked to nurse the baby in the cradle.

I do not know yet what my name is, only that I have an easy heart.

When I crawl out of my nest of pillows my feet look like feet again and the walls have stopped pulsing.

I stand and wobble. I step across a field of browning apples, each with one or two bite marks, scattered like small bruised fruit in an orchard. I totter and hold onto the walls. I open the door and it is dark. Maybe the night is approaching or leaving, I'm not sure. It's either going to get darker or lighter and this is so amusing my boneless body folds into a sitting position and I laugh. A white gull skitters along the sand and laughs with me. Very funny, I say out loud and then notice a slice of pink streaking across the dark sky. It's dawn. I've been here twenty-four hours.

I come inside and pee, brush my teeth, comb my hair. I carefully apply oil all over my body as if I am about to marry, because I am.

I pick up the phone and call Richard. Yes I say, yes. I will. I do.

Nancy London

# We Hold Hands and Jump

RICHARD PULLS INTO MY yard driving a twenty foot U-Haul. He emerges grinning, hands me a hot cup of coffee, sweet the way I like it, and begins lifting my bed, tv, dining room table and six chairs, kitchen pots and pans, end tables and lamps inside the truck while I carefully wrap dishes, glassware and too many vases in newspaper. I give away three dozen house plants to the few group members who are brave enough to stand around and say goodbye. Wendy comes and takes me aside. Feed him well, she offers as parting advice, and I promise I will. The guru had pounded on my front door the night before, rain lashing the trees, unsteady on his feet, drunk for the first time I could recall. I did not let him in.

Later that night in a diner twenty miles down the coast, I sit across from Richard in a booth by the front window where he can keep an eye on our vehicles. I had followed the U-Haul in my little Toyota, and now suddenly I am shaking with anxiety, terrified that I am consigning myself to hell for the next five incarnations.

I'm sorry, I say. I can't do this, it's a mistake. I'm sorry.

His warm brown eyes unblinking, steady, no recrimination.

Okay, he says, pushing the keys to the twenty foot U-Haul monster across the table. But here's the deal. You have to drive yourself back.

The waitress comes around again on her squeaky white sneakers and refills our coffee then stands poised with her pad and pencil. "Ready?"

I take in a breath to last a lifetime, enough oxygen to carry me over the chasm of this moment. Exhale to a slow count of ten. The half-moon breaks through the clouds and spills onto the table, everything illuminated. I push the keys back across the table and nod. "Ready."

We put everything in storage, hold hands and jump into fast moving waters, the guru at our backs threatening black magic, threatening the damnation of our souls, predicting endless misery. The current sweeps us out to sea, past dolphins and breaching whales waving us on.

This is not falling in love. This is plummeting toppling tumbling. This is falling like the tallest tree crashing in the redwood forest. This is falling like a chainsaw cutting me off by the roots.

We land waterlogged, disoriented on a Hawaiian island out in the middle of a vast unending blue. *Where am I?* And the sea answers, *you are here. Breathe. Eat mangoes. Eat papayas. They will heal your womb. Walk on the beach. Swim and swim some more.*

We stay with friends in a small house with a plumeria tree in the yard; after two weeks of a three week vacation, we sell our return tickets and find a place of our own.

Richard's long legs tan as he trades his mainland clothes for skimpy. He builds a gazebo and hangs a hammock out on the deck, then hammers together a bird feeder that brings song to our mornings; he erects a clothes line so I can watch the ocean swell while I pin up the sheets.

He cooks for me when I am too numb to know I am hungry, too overcome with lingering fear that I have made a horrible mistake. And when I cry and say the babies always fall out of my body, he reassures me, says not this one.

We walk the half mile to the beach every morning and again at dusk, gathering the mangoes the wind knocks down, peeling and eating them all at once, diving into the water to wash the sticky sweet juice from our hands and arms. I am coming home to my body, my skin turning brown, my lungs expanding underwater. The turtles take me far from shore to show me their secret caves and hiding places.

Our life slows to no time, to out of time, to this is our time. Time to gather ourselves back into a whole cloth, mend the tears in the fabric where doubt and fear had ripped the seams, bind it together with the gentle touch of trade winds and morning fog. With the sound of waves that lull me to sleep into dreams of a safe place.

Our bodies fit together like the last two long lost pieces of a puzzle, the dissolving warmth of our limbs entwined, reassuring me that I have not spit on pure love, that perhaps I might have even chosen it.

We are married by the local kahuna in a small Hawaiian church with bright blue walls. In the only wedding picture we have we are beaming, draped in leis of plumeria, and above the altar a sign reads *Aloha Ke Akua*, God is Love.

THE RIPENING | Water

# Part Three

---

## BLOOM

Nancy London

# Borderlands

I MARRIED RICHARD, the kindest man I had ever known. But did he know I lived inside my own kingdom? About the years in my small childhood bedroom where I stashed enough chocolate for a twelve hour siege, sealed off from the family chaos down below. Did he know about the border of my skin, saying yes sure I'll take off my clothes but here's the secret: there's a border inside you will not know how to cross because I do not yet know how to find it on the map of my scars.

My heart was in a birdcage grabbing the bars, grabbing strangers. *Pssst* there's the key on the table. Get it. Let me out. It should have been simple but it wasn't.

I knew what it felt like to be inside my own country — the line of trees, the river marking my territory. I never minded the solitude. I knew how to walk the trails, fish for trout, find berries in the fall, whistle to the birds that landed like dreams, like hope, on my outstretched palm.

I knew the old stories and sang them as I rocked myself to sleep.

Slowly, slowly, he rowed up the river and sent an arrow over the wall.

Would you like to dance? He called to me.

Sure, I said, venturing out. No harm in dancing.

Would you let me hold you close? He asked.

Sure, I said. I've been here before.

Would you let me love you, care for you, cherish you, cook for you, give you my seed? Raise a child with you, make money, go broke, make more money, make art, make bread. Make love. What do you say, do you want to dance?

Oh shit, I said. I thought you meant *dance*.

I do, he said. I mean the tango, the surrender into each other's rhythms, each other's scent, our joys and sorrows. I mean the dance that will dance us across borders, across the space where you are you and I am I. I mean dance until there's just a union of opposites, a fiery yin yang that circles through shadow and light until death do us part. I mean hey, do you want to dance?

I wish I could say I said yes. I said maybe, wounded child that I was. But slowly I crept closer, let the beat of the dance move me, began to crave his scent, the weight of him sleeping next to me. Slowly I crept closer until the dust on my knees, on my elbows, under my tongue was the dust of the borderlands I had silently crossed in the night.

Nancy London

# Holy Holy

OH HOLY DAYS and nights of motherhood, breasts finally engorged, wrapped in a sarong, barefoot, brown skin. I inhabit my body, my cells are humming. I cradle my baby who is fussy, who wants me all day and all night and I give myself over to her desire, a desire I have not known until now, driven not by lust and sorrow, but by life force and sunshine pouring in the window as we rock, as I sing her the lullaby my mother sang to me, sing my baby into her body, sing myself back into my original happy body. No mirrors in the house because I am beautiful now, eyes wide open, body spilling joy and song as we crawl across the carpet. One day baby will rise up on sturdy legs and hold onto my little finger, baby dressed in roses and hibiscus, whale song and starlight. I see myself reflected in the eyes of my baby, my laughter the sound of a thousand dark years sent back into the night.

Nancy London

## Across the Universe

You have to burrow down through my astrological chart - Sun in Leo, Cancer rising, Moon in Gemini to get to the hard core five planets in Virgo tucked into the back pocket of the sky. I tell you this because these planets rule my relationship to the Great Mystery. They ground me, turn my eyes to earth, to the plants that need water, the floors that beg to be swept.

When my daughter was young, she and I would ask her smart daddy to explain how the earth revolved around the sun, and so to illustrate, he would bring out a stick, an orange and a lemon and move them around the solar system like a ballet dancer. She and I would hold hands, whisper like bad girls.

Do you understand?

No.

Do you?

We smiled, said thank you. But months later one of us would ask another planetary question and out would come the stick, and now maybe two oranges and two lemons, or a lime if one were around.

We'd hold hands. Shit. The stick. The oranges.

Yeah. Don't ask that again.

It's not that I am not stunned stupid looking up at the night sky. I am. I tilt my head back until my neck hurts and I make the same *ooh aah* noises everyone else is making. But then I think how nice it would be to have tea ready when they come inside, necks stiff from craning, and so I conjure the domestic alchemy of water and herb, bee sugar and fire, and it is a mystery that something so wonderful, so simple as hot tea should be there, radiant as a universe.

Another mystery: how two people fall into the same black hole together, agreeing to cleave to each other like uranium or plutonium before the fission, before critical mass will rip them apart. How the great mystery of love slowly works its way into their blood, taming the wild, the impatient, the cruel, softening the tongue, easing the pain.

Look up, for love has arrived.

Look inside, for nothing else can mend you.

Fall on your knees in the face of the one true mystery of life - the song of the spheres, the dance of the planets as they two-step past each other, the raucous laughter of the gods who travel through space to arrive just in time to heal us with the power of love.

Nancy London

# And Then There Was Fear

Fear lived in the basement, in the deep freeze. He'd come out when I was alone, touch me, turn me to ice.

"You know no one's home, right? They're all dead. Gone. Poof." He leaned against the stove, turned on a burner, let the ice melt off his fingers, pool into a puddle on the floor.

He laughed, a sound like dry thunder on the horizon. "Don't worry about the puddle. Your mother's not coming home. You're all mine."

"And my father?" I croaked.

"Oh, he's long gone, honey. You'll never see him again." Fear grinned, so cold and sharp I took a deep breath and couldn't let it out for many many years.

Yes he died.

Yes I never saw him again.

Yes I froze, so small, so open, so in love and in need of this big man in the three piece suits and the gray fedora hat.

"See?" fear says now when my husband goes off to hike. "See? See that? He's leaving. He's never coming back."

I follow Richard out to the car. "Text me when you know where you're going. Do you have water? Is your phone charged? Can I pack you some snacks?"

Sometimes I stand there holding him back, my hand on the bumper, and I burst into tears.

"It happened before," fear says. "It can always happen again. In fact, it probably *will* happen again. Someday. No. This day. Today.

"Today the phone will ring and a police-y voice will say 'Is this Nancy London?' and you'll hang up and run into the closet, throw up behind the shoes and eat all the candy bars you've hidden. Oh, right. That's what you did when you were twelve.

"Now you'll say 'Who's asking?' and a guy will say "Ma'am this is the Santa Fe police and we've got some bad news for you' and you'll say 'she's not here.' You'll hang up and then sit very still because if you can sit still then it didn't happen.

"You and me, kid," fear says. "Just like old times. Remember the years we hung out together? The trouble we got into? Everyone thought you were such a bad kid but I knew the truth. You were running from fear hahaha big joke because I was your ride into the city. I was the bartender serving Black Russians to a thirteen year old. I was everyone who loved how available, how open, how pleasing you were. But it was all me, fear licking your toes and making it all better, because if for one moment you felt how close we were, if you knew from the first moment your daddy didn't come home what kind of hell you'd be burning in without him, shit girl, you ought to thank me for numbing you up real good and taking you for a ride.

"Say thank you," fear says, chucking me under the chin with an icicle finger.

"Fuck off," I say. "Richard will come home. He's not going to die today. This is different. I can't stand here in the driveway weeping for a death that hasn't even happened."

"Are you sure?" he asks, raising an eyebrow.

"No. Not sure."

"So then?"

So then I do all the everythings I've learned to do when I'm paralyzed by fear. Four breaths in. Hold. Four breaths out. Hold. Repeat until my heart stops stampeding across my chest looking to break out of the corral.

Dance. Sweat my prayers. Sweat out fear like it's poison, which it is.

Stop before I eat the entire carton of chocolate ice

cream, always so friendly, always willing to numb me back to the Stone Age.

Make soup. Re-pot my geraniums. Let my hands linger in dirt, in life. On the keyboard.

Stay close to anything that makes me glad to be alive.

Light candles on my altar. Pray that when the time comes to answer that phone call, I'll have nourished enough happiness to handle suffering. I'll have settled my score with fear. I'll be battered and torn apart, surrendered to the holy fire of grief where fear and doubt sizzle and burn. I'll be barefoot, walking through the radiant flame of love that never dies.

# Addictions

By the time I was a few years out of diapers, I was addicted to sugar. It was the only way I knew how to regulate my nervous system before I understood I had a nervous system that needed regulating. All I knew was that the adults were unpredictable; sometimes smiling, sometimes raging, and I did not know which face I'd meet when I entered a room. Sugar calmed my pounding heart, elevating me several floors above the fear that nibbled away at my brain.

Sugar made everything okay.

I stole candy from the corner drug store, panhandled for spare change at the local movie theater, helped myself to a few of the dollar bills in my mother's wallet. I traded the carefully wrapped tuna and pickle sandwiches in my school lunch box for Twinkies.

At various times I've been addicted to cigarettes, pot, sex, and despite everything I know about nutrition - occasionally, still, sugar.

But lately I've uncovered another addiction, swimming silently in the black bottom waters of my psyche. I'm addicted to appeasement, to people- pleasing, to accommodation. To self-sacrifice. Saying *yes I'd love to see you* saying *oh really how interesting* saying *yes tell me more.*

This may sound like good manners, like being a good friend, but under all that smile and shimmer is the child who feared unpredictable rage, ice cold withdrawal, punishment because Mama was having a really bad day. The child who learned to read the weather report on the face of the adults, learned to smile, to joke, to offer an arm, a leg, anything to feed the narcissistic beast. A child who learned to betray herself and hide in plain sight.

I became a master at rescuing others from their own discomfort. I've eaten meals when I wasn't hungry with people I didn't like. I've had sex with men who wanted me, and who I was afraid of offending by saying no. Three of them showed up in my dream last night just in case I needed a reminder about how accommodating I could be.

So. I'm working on it, but it's hard. Holding to a boundary means resisting the burning impulse to take it all back. Setting a boundary means feeling the anxiety the appeasement was meant to avoid. Feeling the anxiety leads to feeling the grief and the rage over having given myself away. *Oh yes really I'd love to see you* (lie) *please come for dinner, honestly, I'm fascinated by your endless self-referring stories,*(bullshit) and *I'll overlook the fact that you never ask how I am* because the child still believes appeasement is the only way to safety.

Wasn't that Chamberlain's hope with Hitler?

It took pot, mushrooms, acid and peyote to find the basement of my being where the bitch lived. The one who didn't give a damn, who couldn't care less about what anyone else was feeling.

Hey, what about me? She was screaming in the dark. What the fuck about me? What? You have something against Jewish girls from Queens who grew up roller skating on cement, who stole all her clothes, tucked candy bars from the drug store in the front side and back pockets of her jeans. What? You're only nice to everyone else?

She had a point. I liked hanging out with her. She hated most of the people I was being nice to and spared no words telling me so. She farted when she got bored in public, ate with her fingers and let the hostess do the dishes.

Listen, I finally had to say, we need to negotiate. Back off a bit. Get some manners for christsake. I promise

I won't shut you down into the basement again, but sheesh, be a bit polite when it's strategic.

She took the gum out of her mouth and pasted it behind her ear. OK she said. Deal for now.

And yes of course my heart has genuine impulses towards love and connection that have nothing to do with people - pleasing. But it means discriminating between the best of me from the survival skills that no longer serve me. I am in the fairy tale castle, sorting grains of rice. What liberates me, what chains me. What makes my heart sing, what shuts me down. Who talks with me, who talks at me. Who do I appease and why.

Look out the castle window and count the stars scratching their way through the coal black night, yearning to shine. Radiant, pulsing, semaphoring the gospel: it's not too late. It's never too late to return home, to greet yourself at the door, to rest awhile in the warmth and comfort of your own true self.

# Unchained Melody

THIS IS MY MOTHER'S STORY: when I was five years old, I went over to our upright Steinway piano and picked out *You Are my Sunshine*.

Did I want to take lessons? She asked.

I did.

Every Saturday morning Mom drove me to Ruth Ettinger's. I'd have a half-hour private lesson and then join a small group of kids about my age. We danced to the beats she clapped out, introducing our feet to rhythm. She'd play three note tunes and we'd sing them back, learning pitch. At the end of every class she'd wind up her piano - shaped music box, and we'd get to pick a cellophane wrapped hard candy.

We staged Gilbert and Sullivan performances in her basement. *The Mikado, H.M.S. Pinafore.* The parents crammed on small chairs at the back of the room while we sang and danced and sweated our way in makeshift costumes across her basement floor. I still sing Nanki

Poo's song when I'm driving.

I loved Ruth and I loved the piano. I practiced and got better. The instrument was becoming a part of my hands; my fingers had found their home. I loved every moment of the eight years I spent with her.

When I was thirteen, one year after my father's death, Mom fired Ruth and hired Mrs. Anslinger at the Long Island Institute of Music. Mom had decided I needed a new teacher, one who would bring more discipline to my playing.

Mrs. Anslinger still had her German accent. She assigned difficult pieces for me to learn, then tasked me with performing them during the Saturday evening concerts put on by the Institute. But my anxiety was so acute that during my third performance I had a dizzy spell and walked off the stage in sweat and shame.

When my fingers got tangled up playing a fast passage, Mrs. Anslinger rapped my knuckles with a ruler.

Fuck you, I said and walked out of my lesson. What she couldn't see was that everything was tangled up, not just my fingers.

I closed the lid on the piano.

Years later, I moved west, to Santa Cruz, into a mountain cabin. The only thing the previous tenant had left behind was a black Steinway. A genie, gleaming and powerful. I used it to hold my extra winter clothes.

But pianos kept showing up, teasing me, a sharp inbreath of recognition, the beauty of the white keys, the lure of the black, offering me a lifetime of nights to do my grieving in.

I moved again, down to the coast. A gorgeous long legged blonde, an Acrosonic Spinet, posed coyly against one wall in the living room. I gave it the cold shoulder. It played *Unchained Melody* trying to seduce me.

Shut up, I said.

But then Bill rolled into town riding his four wheel gypsy wagon. We met at an evening meditation on the chakras. He asked if I'd like to see the inside of his van. Of course I would. Thick Persian rugs, a cook stove with a pot of chai on simmer. And a piano. He played. He sang. He seduced me that night in his cave where the music was as thick as the hash we smoked.

He parked outside my small seaside bungalow, and most nights I'd follow him down the rabbit hole and listen to the music that flowed spontaneously from him.

Play, he said.

I don't play, I said.

You do, he said.

No. The music's gone, I said. It was rapped out of my knuckles and beat out of my heart.

Play.

I played. Not Chopin, not Rachmaninoff, not all the

complex contrapuntal whiz bang pieces I played at concerts while sweat poured down my sides. I played what flowed from my heart onto the keys.

Not bad, he said. Not bad at all.

I moved up to a small town in the mountains so that I could sit at the lotus feet of a good looking emotionally stunted guru. And yes of course my new home had a piano left behind.

I played.

I bought my own piano when I moved again. Now I play before I write. It's how I know how I feel.

If you listen at the door and the waves are moving in E flat minor, don't knock. I'm grieving my ancestors and all those I have loved and lost.

C Sharp? Maybe. Leave a note.

A Minor. Leave a latte and a croissant and don't come back.

The standard rock and roll C Am F G? I'm singing *Hallelujah* with Leonard Cohen, maybe thinking about how nice it would be to fuck him, so definitely go away.

This is my wordless offering to the god of words. The mute soaring notes that say Here I am. I'm sad I'm scared I'm hopeful I am so bloody glad to be alive today. I am here asking for inspiration and guidance and all I have to give you is my song.

# Home

WHEN MY MOTHER locked the front door of my childhood home for the last time, she might as well have doused it with kerosene and lit a match. Every report card and award that said how smart I was, every pencil line on the door frame marking my growth, every homemade valentine my little hands had liberally sprinkled with glitter...Mommy I love you! poof. All gone.

She was kicking up dust, getting fitted in minks and diamonds, ready for a marriage that would take her away on a European honeymoon while I moved in with a strange girl who smelled like cheese for my first year of college.

I did not have the vocabulary or the skill or the courage to say *how will I find you? Where is home now? Would someone please hold me?*

What could I rescue from the flames? All my diaries gone to garbage collection along with the clothes I had outgrown. No sentimental relics from my babyhood, no booties, not even a photo album in a box to be shipped to her new home when she returned. Even my beloved Steinway piano sold to a Russian who came and trucked it away before I could play one last Moonlight Sonata.

What could I stuff in my pockets? Gravel from the driveway where I let my boyfriend explore my body until the porch light came on and I was hauled inside?

Could I preserve a dogwood blossom from the tree that broke out in astonishing beauty every spring, white against red brick, green glinting with dew. Could I take just that?

Or maybe a branch from the weeping willow tree my mother sat under that hot summer when she was nine months pregnant with me, her swollen feet in a bucket of ice water, she a goddess of girth and contentment, for one sweet moment her sorrows softened by the shade of a weeping tree.

Could I take the heat that choked my upstairs bedroom, or the way the snow tumbled in fat flakes past the street lamp or the sound of my roller skates on concrete or oh please yes, maybe somehow I could stuff in my college suitcase the look on my father's face as he let go of the two wheeler the night I rode off on my own down the street and then back, beaming, beaming, falling into his open arms.

None of that could I take. None of that came with me. Only this: a round stone from the cold stormy sea where my grandmother taught me to swim.

I carry it with me always, and place on every windowsill in every home I have ever made.

But still. There is a home I am searching for that remains out of sight, just over the rise, beyond the bend. It is a place of peace and forgiveness where the small one inside of me can finally rest, curl up in her own bed, turn the light off knowing she's safe. And maybe I will walk across deserts dragging a tattered hope behind me like a much loved doll, looking for this home, always out of reach, always just around the next curve.

And maybe it is the despair of the world I am feeling, a yearning for peace and safety for our families, a home where our children can grow up rooted on land that has been tended for generations by our ancestors.

Maybe it is the agony of displacement, of watching it all go up in flames, that brings me to my knees each morning in prayers for peace. For the sweet, simple comfort of a home we can all return to at the end of the day and be greeted by warmth, by safety, by laughter and the familiar smells of food cooked with love. Maybe my longing is the longing of a world wanting only to go home to a place where we are each other's trusted neighbors.

I have wandered, been uprooted by wind and fate and the imperative to keep seeking, across time and borders, a place that feels like home. And now when I do not know where I am, I rest my head on my beloved's chest, because what I long for I left so long ago with nothing in my pockets except the grief from a small child's bedroom, the scent of a blossom, the echo of a lullaby remembered in my dreams. When all I have is a stone from a stormy sea anchoring me to the past I rest my head on his chest and say – you are my home, and in that one still moment it is comfort enough.

# Dialogue With Our Dreams

ONE HOT JULY WEEKEND in the dreamtime that was the 70s, my girlfriend Sara and I hitchhiked down Highway One in Big Sur and snuck into Esalen because the great Fritz Perls was giving a demonstration of Gestalt Therapy, his new theory of dream interpretation. He asked for a volunteer, and Sara raised her hand.

Two chairs up on the small platform, she sat in one while the second remained empty. At his prompting, Sara recounted a dream that involved a city street and some gum stuck to the bottom of her shoe. He stopped her when this detail twanged his intuition.

"Sit in the other chair," he commanded. "Be the gum on the bottom of your shoe."

And the gum spoke to Sara, told her all kinds of things about her low self-esteem, and everyone clapped and Fritz probably took the sweetest morsel back to his bed that night, Fritz reeking of the cigars he always chewed, his sweat, the acrid odor of his belief in his own brilliance.

I think about dream interpretation when I wake from the prosaic ones I often have now. Details about getting ready for a trip, or what kinds of art supplies my husband is running out of. I lie in bed and laugh, thinking of Fritz, refusing his otherworldly invitation to dialogue with my shopping list, refusing to listen to it tell me I eat too much dairy.

Then there are the nights I go to bed with a heavy heart. Some weight, some anchor pulling me to the ocean floor. I am sinking, waterlogged, teary, but I don't know why. I close my eyes and ask to be taken to the place of magic where I am free from the mundane details of a long-married life.

And then. I am sitting on the little stone wall with a coyote at my feet, looking at the house I grew up in.

Oh, I say. We are here again. My grandmother sits beside me, nuzzles the coyote, puts her arm around me.

They're all here, she says, her Yiddish accent thick enough to lick like ice cream. And then my parents come out the front door and they are so young and I see how beautiful and in love they were for that one crystalline moment. He's looking at her so tenderly, like he always did, trying to capture her attention like a firefly in a jar, and she's happy, bundling her big winter coat around her small frame, and I see that they were happy, and for that one moment, so very beautiful.

    I want to see more but I wake. I have been crying. My pillow is wet. I feel emptied out like a bowl tipped over. I lie still and bring them all back with me, out of the dream into the day where I set them down in the red earth of the desert, bring water, bring song.

Nancy London

# Enemies

My Aunt Ethel could stop a stampeding herd of elephants by placing her hands on her hips and snorting, *Oh Please*.

Who wouldn't be silenced, shamed, swallowing the words that threatened to break loose from a parched throat?

*Oh Please.* Enemies? What's with enemies? Who are your enemies? Who did you so bad you didn't survive? Tell me.

I try. I look back, but to tell you the truth I'm at that stage of life where I have paid therapists enough to cover their mortgages, divorces and yoga retreats in Bali in order to work through my enemy shit, so when I look back I see…what? A battlefield strewn with the wounded, much as I was wounded. I see people groping for each other with claws instead of hands. I see fire flaming from open mouths. Scorched earth policy instead of words of comfort.

So okay. My mother. As alluring and toxic as the

poison red apple. Right. But her mother tried to abort her with a coat hanger when she was in utero. Try to imagine being that tiny fetus. What tenderness might be left in your heart? What milk of kindness might you have flowing in abundance for your own small child?

It is an old story. The witch in the crumbling house tries to snuff out the light of the sunny girl child, but she always fails. The child finds the key that opens the cage where the magic bird lives, the one who sings the song of finding the road home.

So my enemy? *Oh Please.* She was my mother. She bled. I could not staunch her wound. I helped her die when she asked me to. I've started wearing her jewelry. There's nothing left to forgive.

Mom comes to me in a dream. Her cheeks are rosy, but her eyes are wild. She asks me to visit her soon. Time is running out. I tell her I can come over spring break for two weeks. Everything feels urgent. She is begging, silently telling me that she is dying.

But wait, I think when I wake up, this dream so real, so much like a visit from her. You're already dead.

What do you want? I ask the faint trail of her that remains.

Mom's voice is filled with the longing I remember. I want you to gather your memories of us, she says. Set the table with the good china and the silver that you'll have to polish. Roast a chicken the way we like it. Small red potatoes. Cold vodka. Chocolate mousse.

What else do you want? I ask.

To celebrate the love we missed while we had the chance. To tell you I'm proud of you, that you were the daughter I always wanted.

And this, she says. To hear you say you forgive me and I will say I forgive you. It's easier now for me as I hope it is for you. Can you tell me you love me despite my rages, my envy? Have you seen deep enough into my wounds to offer me the compassion I need to heal?

I want to be cherished, she says. To be understood. Light a candle for me, for us, and keep it burning. Be extravagant. Light two. Light three. Let them blaze all day, bright enough to rival the sun.

Can you? Will you?

Yes, Mama, I say to the lingering breath of her perfume in the air, my heart a full moon on a warm summer night. I can. I will.

Nancy London

# Besotted and Bedazzled

I LONGED FOR A SOULMATE. I confessed this to my soul many years ago on a night when the sky was a blackboard and I wrote my wishes upon it.

She looked up from her knitting, her large jungle green eyes. Aren't I enough?

Well, I said, kind of, but you know, I get cold at night. I get lonely. I hear there's a big *big* love out there just waiting. Eternal love. Transcending time and space. The besotted and bedazzled *always no one else but you.*

She came and sat beside me. Placed her warm hands on my trembling heart. Oh kiddo, she said kindly. You poor thing. You are asking for what only a god can provide. But ok. Here's bread for the journey and a twenty if you need to call a cab.

Into the woods, onto the seashore, across scalding deserts, I set out dressed all in white, a crown of flowers in my hair. No map, just the faint prints left in the sand by the barefoot seekers before me.

The first years tumbled and toughened me. My dress got dirty, the flowers withered and died, fallen by the wayside. My hands, my feet, my innocent young girl burned up in a pyre.

But then. But then. I met and married my beloved and holy shit it was hard. We fought like alley cats. We hurtled words hot as lava. We threatened and wept. Gradually I learned to hold back my asp tongue before the fast strike, before regrets. We survived, cautiously drew in our claws, began to listen to each other instead of pulling the pin on the grenade.

But yesterday I woke up missing my old self. I was tired of being and having a soulmate, always rubbing the hard edges off each other, always ready to point out the hubris, the inconsistencies, the plain daily pain in the assness of dirty socks on the floor and dishes left in the sink. I felt snappish, critical.

I had wanted passion, the emotional and spiritual intensity of a committed relationship, but had been dumb blind to what it would ask of me, how it would transform the very fabric of my being.

My soul had by now knitted several dozen afghans and watched quietly from the corner.

Told you so, she said. Told you it would be hard. No lovey dovey all day all night. Just the dirty work of getting down to loving each other in all your shadow and light. The hard work of seeing the other as yourself.

Yeah, well, I need a timeout.

I began planning a trip to the coast to see a friend. Refused dinner.

Then it was bedtime. My husband fell like a brick into dreamworld while I chewed my cuticles.

Wake up, I finally said around midnight.

He bolted awake. What? What happened?

I'm upset. I want to run away. This soulmate shit is too hard.

Now you tell me, he laughed. After all these years?

Don't laugh, I said, jamming my finger into his rib.

Don't hurt me, he said.

I will if I want to.

Ok, I was five years old, passing in and out of love faster than a pinwheel sparkler. I was needing something I couldn't name, some freedom, some time to spin with the planet turning from spring to summer, time to have coffee with a stranger. Nothing but time to dance under the sweet soft jazz of the full moon. I wanted to kick off my shoes and wander the earth looking for Buddha in a dappled shade forest. I wanted to hear him say *what took you so long?*

I hated you today, I said, and we laughed.

And then for the next two hours we hashed it out… how he felt when I said X. Why he said Y. How he feels pressured, how I feel invisible. The same fight we've been having only now it's been transistorized. We are both quicker to say *I know. I do that. I'm sorry.* Our outbursts of outrage tempered with laughter that float above the bed like fairy dust.

And then it's all been said. We agree we have both been wrong and both been right.

And there it was. The conflict that has followed me, defined me in this lifetime, in the lifetimes before this one that I have glimpsed in dreams and altered states. I need to be alone. I need to be with my mate. One lifetime alone in a field of wild plants, a botanist, on my own, free of commitments, no children, no chores. And then the loneliness and yearning that pulled me into the next life: mother of six, wife lover baker songmaker, the work of sustaining a family all consuming, yearning for a taste of alone.

Alone. Together. But never alone together.

Alone together that does not swallow me until I need to break out, take a hammer to the adobe walls of our union so that I might pick through the rubble, gather the ash- covered pieces of my long abandoned self and bolt for the light.

Now I follow the hieroglyphics of love, like bird tracks in sand. A relationship so long together you have to wonder if the binding will hold, or if the glue will become soft and crumble like the spine of a well-loved book of poetry.

The days and nights when love feels dried up and threatens to blow away on this hot desert wind, when all that is left is habit and the routine of what shall we have for dinner.

And then the magic of touch on a barely cooled down night with the covers thrown off, our bodies hollowed out from covid, from sleepless weeks and fevers and bad dreams and then finding each other again through touch, like braille, like reading the book of love backwards to the beginning.

The years rolling back, the laughter returning, remembering the other as our mate, remembering desire, remembering how the body moves when it is moved, and the now thank you breeze coming through the window cooling our fevers, dispelling the anger and boredom, helping our fingers find the pulse of our longing, dissolving the restlessness, stirring us awake with the magic of love renewed.

Nancy London

# Small Deaths

IT WAS CHRISTMAS and our daughter was packing. She was flying away to marry her love, an Australian man she had met in Ireland the year she turned eighteen, the year she and her girlfriend rented a moldy apartment in Galway, the year she hardly wrote, but sent me two sweaters bought with her meager salary as a barista. The card did not say holy shit I miss you; it only said life is good. How are you?

I'm not sure how we managed, just the two of us rattling around, the house empty of her laughter. Even the sidewalk chalk turtle washed away that year.

It was Christmas and it was snowing, big fat snowflakes slowly falling, all her stuffed animals in boxes in the closet, nothing in her suitcase but stardust and hurry up and I don't want to miss my plane and goodbye goodbye tossed over her shoulder.

I drove her to the airport, and we were silent most of the way, the only sound the rough grinding of my heart like it was slipping a gear. At Southwest she pecked my cheek, said she loved me, would take care, write often, hopped out at the curb, slung her backpack over her shoulder and disappeared into the crowd.

I could not bear turning on the radio driving home. Just my two hands raw from the cold, gripping the steering wheel, every emotion so close to the surface, and snow still falling.

When I got home I could not find Richard anywhere so I pushed my feet back into my boots and went looking.

I found him in the pickup wrapped in a sleeping bag, nearly frozen to death. This man who had faced down his Mormon demons for too many years, doing the hardest work of all excavating and befriending the shadows that had followed him since childhood, this man filled with faith and kindness had finally met one death too many - the I don't really need a daddy anymore death, the thank you and goodbye death of a daughter he had caught as she flew from my body 18 years ago.

Honey, come inside, I said softly, because I did not want to startle him, because he would snap break shatter if I moved too fast, if I spoke too loud.

Honey, come inside, I said again, and led him to our bed where I warmed him with my breath and my body.

Later that night, an old gypsy dressed in rags came to visit. The air crackled and flared, the wind howled and the snow drifts grew deeper. She invited me outside into the cold, which was her home.

Those fools, those saints, she said, they make it sound like the dark night of the soul is cozy, candles to light the way, the kettle always on, a yearning in the heart. But who doesn't have a yearning in the heart.

I bring the other kind of dark night. The one that will freeze you, she said. The one that smells like burnt paper and dried leaves. Do you understand? She asked. You have entered the faraway land where you will travel alone across frozen ground, seeking shelter from a cold that is cruel even by saintly standards.

We don't write poems here, she said. We don't go out into the soft fragrant night looking for the Holy Beloved. We pile up blanket upon blanket so that when morning comes we can move our limbs, make food, go to work, return home and tend to the one who will journey through his own personal hell month after month as you grow solid as ice.

And that is how it happened. Richard journeyed through a dark night alone while I looked on helpless. I kept him warm. I cooked our meals. But he was gone to me as he worked through the demons that were dancing, insisting on his attention, taunting him, whispering of his failures and lack of favor in God's eyes.

I often grew impatient, wanting him to return to

me whole, but my anger drove him deeper into the shadows and afterwards filled me with shame. When I left for work, off attending to my hospice patients, it was a guilty relief to be gone. When I returned, it felt like taking the night shift. I lost myself in the routine and survived by becoming frozen to my own needs and cold to his, just as the gypsy had predicted.

Listen. How do I tell you this story without also telling you that this was a brutal descent into deeper layers of unconditional love than anything I had imagined when I had gone looking for a teacher of pure love? How do I say that when those months were over and my beloved emerged back into daylight having turned his demons into art, his shadow into friend and his fear into fuel, I had seen the cruelty of my own cold silence and was transformed. How do I tell you that for better or worse became better, much better, as the air shattering sound of my grief melted the ice and my wail brought back the sun.

# Mama Said There'd Be Days Like This

Mama said there'd be days like this:

days when you crack open one eye and the slate gray sky is pushing through the window, and your demons have let themselves in the back door and are sitting at the foot of your bed thumbing through the photo album of all your regrets, pointing them out one by one, waiting to tell you that in a past lifetime you were the fire keeper and you let the flame go out.

days when a murder of crows lands on your roof demanding answers and you think you're supposed to apologize but you can't remember for what.

days when the child in you is on a hunger strike for nothing but sugar, and the fragment you are trying to grab from your dream last night that whispered instructions from your ancestors has dissolved along with the melody you're still straining to hear.

days when all your good intentions affirmations visualizations donations and inspirations have declared a time out and are sitting around a card table drinking Irish whiskey, while shame is circling the room, ready to pounce.

days that ask us, despite the storm, to get up and step out onto the broken ground of dysfunction, to create the world anew by telling a story, one that helps make sense of the chaos, a story that will rekindle our spirit and ease our soul.

new stories about how there is no outrunning the shadows that pursue us, how to turn and welcome them home, bring them water, a warm place to rest, sing them the lullaby we learned from our mother's mother, ask where it hurts and listen.

stories about how our tears water the ground and how the garden that blooms there restores us to life.

stories that reconnect us to the living pulse of the natural world and the underlying wholeness of life, about the crows and jays, the flickers and finches, that invite us to notice we are not alone, have never been alone, and when we ask for help it always arrives.

new stories about the radiant world beckoning us to slip out of our minds and into her open arms, how when we put our finger on the pulse of her one beating heart, we find the rhythm of our own wild, and how dancing breaks a sweat that breaks the trance.

the story of how to see beauty despite the destruction, how wonder and suffering live side by side, how laughter is the doorway to the divine.

story by story we are spooning our words into the baby bird mouths of the warriors who, may it be so, will grow weary of blood and the cry of revenge and want only to lie under the willow and hear the old songs as they pass down through the soft mouths of women.

this is the story of how everything we do is sacred, how each moment of joy is precious, each touch a healing. The story of the bonds between us that cannot be broken, of the hate that will burn itself out and the love that will flare up, incandescent like the phoenix, and sink its teeth into our hearts and refuse to let go.

Nancy London

# Breasts

I wore my breasts like they were a prize I had been given for a contest I didn't remember entering.

Pure round orbs, the children of the goddess moon, they arose as mountains rise out of the sea - perfect, whole, so firm and luscious they struck awe in me.

What do I do with you? I whispered.

Clothe me, they said, until you are older.

And then older, the delight I took in pulling up my shirt, flashing them, daring, laughing. These were the 60s, the 70s, bare breasts were everywhere. I have pages in my photo album of me with a wild grin, holding up my shirt, exposing my high beams, my headlights, the flashlight I turned on to find my way home in the dark.

I never show these pictures to my husband. He'd want to know who took them, and then wouldn't want to hear the list of wild coyote men who touched me with their hot fevered hands, who brought me to my knees wet and moaning.

And then?

Then they filled with milk, flowered, bloomed, redefined beauty in preparation for a child.

Oh, I said in awe. So *that's* what you are made for. And my baby latched on and sucked. I fed her from these breasts that had undone grown men who still called at night and hung up when my husband answered the phone.

Waves of milk and honey that my breasts gave to my child, a river of sweet holy sacrament, a never ending feast of love between us that time will not dry up.

And now?

Now there is a scar on my right breast where the tumor was removed. Now I fall asleep cradling my breast as I once cradled my child. I speak softly to it when the lights are out and my husband stirs in his sleep beside me.

Shush I say. Everything is okay. We are here. We are intact. We almost lost you but here we are and we laugh because the fullness is gone, the moon has sunk below the horizon and we are laughing softly as all aging women must laugh.

But we had our day, didn't we, I say, as I rub the scar, tender the scar that speaks now not of passion but of survival, and we remember the wild dance naked under the full moon, and we remember feeding our child, and we remember how frightened we were that one of us would end up in the surgeon's bucket.

But we are here, they whisper back. We are together and now we snuggle and hum and say thank you for the light of the moon and the heat of the sun and for the weight we have carried on our chest like a treasure, like a birthright, like the bounty of a queen.

Nancy London

# Beauty Stepped into the Room

I sat alone in my room with the mirrors covered, mourning the end of youth, the end of the shine that had brought all the suitors to me bearing promises like roses blooming.

I know it is futile, but still, when I'm in a department store, I pick up a handful of cosmetic samples and bring them home with some degree of hope springing eternal. Maybe this unique combination of ingredients - some foreign long chain chemical, some animal urine or hummingbird drool will be the magic bullet to fill in the cracks and fissures on my face, bless me with new rejuvenated skin so that I can keep running from the inevitability of aging.

But really, my face would need a motor oil infusion to see much of a difference.

I covered the mirrors so I would not have to look, but Beauty stepped into the room.

What are you doing? she asked. Why are you turning away?

I saw that she was old, still wearing the same green dress she had worn in youth, the same rose tucked behind her ear. The same bells around her ankles like the laughter of small children. The gypsy earrings.

You grew old, I said, and went to uncover a mirror so she could see for herself.

She stopped my hand.

Don't, she said. I no longer look. I refuse to see the lie.

What lie? I asked.

The lie that beauty dies.

But you are old, I protested, tears streaming down my face. You will grow older and more wrinkled.

She cut me off.

Of course I will, child. Did you think your beauty would last forever? Did you want to stay bound to what the mirror shows you? Did you think that your days as a ruler of men could be stretched with peptides, laser treatments, derma planing and chemical peels strong enough to strip varnish? Aerobics, green drinks, seasonal fasting, silver nitrate, oxygen bars, multivitamins, face lifts, leg lifts, boob lifts, tummy tucks and pussy tighteners?

She laughed so hard I was transfixed by her light.

It spilled into the room and lit up the dust motes. It rang through the forest and brought the crows and coyotes to her feet. It rained down on the green grass and caused the worms to turn in pleasure.

Her laughter brought the sun and the stars into alignment, raised the thunder and the wind gods. Her laughter shook the planets loose until her radiance lit up the world all around me.

She placed her hand on my aching heart until all the beauty I feared had been lost came tumbling out. The beauty of friendship and forgiveness. Of patience and the renewal of faith. Of health after illness. Of love burning steady and bright as the stars. Of the wisdom to age well and with grace.

Behold! she said. Beauty all around you. Beauty inside you. Beauty young and dazzling as a thousand new moons.

Nancy London

# Dreamtime

It was my favorite ritual from the young time with our daughter - she'd come into the kitchen and she and her daddy would share their dreams. They were both big dreamers. They flew. They soared. They had initiations from power animals - the jaguar, the radiant deer, the meandering turtle. I'd be at the stove making breakfast, listening to my family listen to each other.

I did not feel left out. I didn't remember my dreams, or if I did, they were the mundane variety - a swim in my favorite ocean, a visit from an old boyfriend come to woo me again.

Our daughter lives in Australia now. But still, she calls and asks to speak with her daddy if I'm the one to answer the phone. I can hear her excitement over the wires. *Dad!!!!! Listen to this dream!*

Or I'll find him at 3 am at his desk, sending her an email, sharing the dream that woke him.

But here's the thing. What I dreamed was this life

with them.

I dreamed a dream that called this family, this man, this child into being with the heady perfume of longing, with the wet desire to push a baby out of my body, dreamed with my breasts that had begun making milk before I conceived.

I longed for them. I called for them. I reached into the dreamworld, through the gauzy veil and pulled them towards me.

The sound of joy like helium rising, daddy singing silly songs with baby on his shoulders, her first laugh a bouquet of roses tossed up in the air.

And later, the sound of birthday parties with children shrieking shoving and cheering when the fairy arrived with the cake.

The sound, oh my god, the sound of joy.

We dreamed together. We dreamed snowfall and mountains, Richard reading us *Lord of the Rings,* road trips with the Beatles, Janis and Joni, trash talking the Gilmore Girls under the quilt. We dreamed mama cat and her kittens on a blanket in the closet. Tell me a story, come put me to bed. Tea parties, popcorn, double dare diving into icy cold rivers.

We dreamed we were just three and we loved so softly, so true.

I see it now, of course. How the life I dreamed for us was made to end. All dreams end. We shake ourselves awake. We say where was I? Was that real? Did I hold that child in my belly? Did I give her life? Where has she gone and why can't I follow?

Where is the family in that small house that I could not wait to leave once she was gone, the walls still vibrating with our laughter, with the smell of toast and jam, the kitchen crowded with her friends lounging about, Richard's cast iron pan sizzling at the stove, the sound of cheese and bean burritos with green chile, passing from hand to hand, the sound of chewing, of teenage girl laughter shy and bold and crazy wise, hungry teenagers who tell me now as married women with children of their own that our kitchen was their safe place, their sanctuary, their island of sanity and acceptance during their turbulent years.

Where is the sofa that just fit against the kitchen wall where we could lie with feet dangling over the edge, chat up the cook, drink the first cup of coffee, watch squirrels outside on the wall, watch mama birds teach their babies how to fly.

I did not know that my child was growing, growing, silently growing, beginning to weave her own dreams apart from us. I did not look. I did not want to know until it was too late and she had dreamed her own soulmate, their farm, the snakes and eagles that call her by name.

We could not follow. She took the unchained melody of our family and opened a window for it to flow into her new home.

And now the coyote comes for the food I leave out for him. He howls under my window. I have the sound of his friendship, his kinship. He crosses my path as I hike and we search each other for clues. Who are you? What are you called?

I am dreaming again, weaving a new story, repairing the web that gave way to give her freedom, and when I sit in silence what I hear is joy. A cathedral bell ringing in the monastery of my heart. Far off, very near.

# Love's Wounds

I TRAVELED THROUGH thickets until I came to a clearing where I found my heart, drinking from the crystal blue waters of eternal life.

I've looked everywhere for you, I said, out of breath.

She appeared tired, and there were wounds in her side.

What happened? I asked, stepping closer to examine the bright red blood that was flowing freely.

I'm wounded, she said simply. It happens. The heart will be wounded if it opens to love.

But who hurt you? I asked, ready to defend her, to find the culprit and exact due punishment.

Who? She laughed softly. There is no shortage of chances for love to lie bleeding.

Do you remember the first primal wound when those tasked with caring for you were not able, were too wounded themselves?

And do you remember the first time you opened yourself body and soul to a lover to find he did not want you as you were? If only you were thinner, quieter or more compliant.

And do you remember the babies you yearned for who did not live long inside your womb?

I remembered.

And then she took my hand and had me feel each scar, name each one, the sorrows and betrayals, the times when someone's best wasn't enough. The endangered species. The no more and the forgotten. The vanishing forests. The droughts and floods and fires. The soft call of trees when they are thirsty.

The endless wars.

But how shall we live, I cried, with all this sorrow?

She showed me how to tend the wounds. Tenderly, tenderly, she kept saying until I got the hang of it, a tender touch on the places that hurt.

We sing the old songs as the world burns, she said, as ash falls, as we drop to our knees in praise and gratitude for what we had, for what we are now losing, for what may only return when our brokenhearted voices rise in sorrow, in praise and in regret.

We return to the world raw, our hearts open because anything less would wither us, she said.

No map, just the compass of the heart. We return to nourish the connections between us, arms around each other, listening deeply to the wounds.

Our love grows strong in the midst of sorrow.

We return knowing where to catch the wind for our next breath, how to hold tight in a storm, where to place our feet so we don't stumble. How to live in a state of not knowing where it is always now and now and now and there's no ledge, no cushion, no wall to lean against. Just letting go laughing and weeping until it hurts.

Drink, my heart said.

I entered the stream and drank from the eternal waters of life. *Love never fails,* she whispered. *Love always wins.*

# Part Four

## RIPEN

# Initiation

Spring arrived battered, her frilly skirt covered in mud from the floods, her petals, delicate as dragonfly wings, torn and shredded from high winds.

But wait, I said. You're supposed to be the symbol of new growth, green shoots pushing up through frozen ground, birds returning to build nests and sing us happy songs.

Spring drank deeply from the water I offered.

That was my younger sister, she said, with no hint of envy. She doesn't live here anymore. This earth, she gestured to the weather-torn landscape, this earth could not support her any longer. Did you think we would sail into another spring and watch the daffodils bloom as if there were no cares in the world?

No. But I hoped we would.

We have crossed a threshold and entered a different season, she said, one we have not lived through before. This is the season of Initiation.

Initiation into what? I asked cautiously.

Haven't you noticed? she asked. People are hurting in new and old ways. More of your friends are ill. More have died.

Yes, I reluctantly agreed. I've noticed. My friends and I had a list of diseases and diagnoses as varied as a six-pack of spring flowers. Tossed about by divorce, death of a loved one, illness, aging, loneliness, addiction, all our habitual ways of being and doing that no longer worked.

Look, she said, I really hate to be a downer, but things have changed.

I could see that.

Do you remember, she asked, when you were a young seeker? How you dressed in white with flowers in your hair, sandalwood at your pulse points, ready to give your all to a guru. This initiation is not that.

You will be broken down and broken open, she continued. Ransacked like a warehouse in a street riot. You will be shipwrecked on the island of your old self, stripped of old ideas of who you are and what you need to survive, no longer willing to say *yes* when you mean *no*, no longer willing to please others before you care for yourself, no longer able to stay silent and hidden in the closet of your childhood despair. No more running blindly into the marketplace, lost in the noise of the crowd when your body weeps for more rest, for comfort.

I'm not sure I like this, I said.

She smiled and tucked a strand of hair behind my ear the way my grandmother did.

No one asks to be pulled into depths you would not willingly choose, she said. But once you step onto the path there is no going back. When the time of initiation is upon you, open to the healing of old wounds and say *yes* - whisper it if you must, simply nod your head in assent. Be willing to let life take from you what it will, because you cannot stop it. But if you let the high winds blow through you and the floodwaters wash you clean, you will find what every seeker has ever sought.

What's that? I asked.

The joy of arriving home to your authentic self, raw and vulnerable, surrendered in the crucible where you will be made whole.

The living pulse of the natural world waiting to receive the gifts you were born to share.

The radiance and power of ten thousand suns warming and opening your tender heart, where choosing love is the question and always the answer.

She placed the first green seeds of faith and renewal in my open palm.

Will you plant them? she asked.

    I will, I said. I will.

Nancy London

## Love Letters

I AM HOUSE SITTING for a friend in a beach town I lived in many many years ago. For one of those years I was young and at a crossroads, a Zen koan - the sound of one girl crying, until the winds swept me along like stardust into the arms of fate where I began the work of befriending my shadow.

I walk these streets now and journey into another dimension while I pick up the pieces I left behind, like seashells, or abalone fragments. The young woman mourning the end of my first marriage and the loss of twins to miscarriage at three months pregnant. My long gone dog that lived to chase sandpipers who I swear is still out there running, hoping. The year when I was lost and grieving and the sea was my mother, rocking me back to life.

I stop at the small bungalow where I lived in that long ago year to take a picture to send to my grown daughter in Australia. *Here. This is where I dreamed of one day being your mother.* A young woman is just about to put her key in the door and graciously steps aside when I ask permission.

I don't understand. How time moved so slowly when my child was young, the days of endless dirty dishes, laundry, what to cook for dinner, and then she was grown and gone and it happened so fast, faster than even the older parents told me it would happen.

Now my friends are dying. They email me and try to sound casual.

Hey, I've had a biopsy and the cancer has returned. Hey, I tried to read the New York Times but the words scrambled and didn't make sense. Hey, the news is bad. Hey, I have to go in for another test. Hey.

Wait. We were just young. Remember the summer we rented that huge house on the shore in Plymouth, 100 rickety wooden stairs down to the beach, no railing, who needed a railing?

Remember the endless hours swanning from one beach blanket to another, sharing joints and warm ice tea, diving into the Atlantic, daring the waves to break us because nothing could break us. Staying up until the rooster crowed, all of us, maybe twenty at any given time, so in love with each other, the babies, the old people, we sang the morning into being, we tucked in the moon. There was no darkness that did not yield to our light and our joy.

And now we write. We say my husband had a stent put in. My daughter's farm was devastated by flood and the fires nearly engulfed her. We say I don't understand how we got so old so fast. We say my wife is dying, we say my eyesight is dimming, we say hey.

Hey I still love you across the miles and when I go for my next MRI I'll text you. Let's not Skype, I look like shit. And we remember going topless, boobs standing at attention, begging to be licked, sucked, begging to be admired because we were young and invincible and we knew it.

We fucking knew it.

We say hey, come talk at my funeral and we laugh. We say you're still beautiful but we laugh again because of the chasm between being beautiful and being still beautiful.

We laugh and say you're full of shit as always.

We say hey, I love you. Thank you for writing this story with me. If you get to the other side before me, be like Houdini. Send down a white feather, a pebble, a seashell, or better yet, a scrap of paper that simply says hey.

We cling to the phone, press it to our ear, cherish what flows between old friends, all the unsaids that are said in the silence. The way we know it's too late in life for regret, who the hell wants to spend even one day in regret when there's still such deep connection, still the breathtaking abundance of the farmers market, a partner who still flirts, and of course the sliver of a hammered silver moon and the desert flowers that stop me to say *if I can bloom, darlin' you can too.*

I retrieve all my missing parts so I can live whole. Wholly. Holy in the moment. So that all my clamoring fears and desires may grow still and know only the surrender to this illuminated presence, and like the fog horns that sound through the night, hear only love calling me home.

# The History of Love

As a precaution before our long flight to see our daughter in Australia, Richard takes a routine stress test on a high powered treadmill and fails. The following week, at the urging of the medical staff, we have an appointment with a heart surgeon, a short man in baby blue scrubs, bald, wide in the butt and hips, who explains open heart surgery to us on a grease board, drawing little parallel lines for arteries and veins with a red grease marker.

What he wants to do is saw open Richard's chest, stop his heart, hook him up to a machine that will keep him alive while he strips a vein from his leg and kind of shoves over another from behind his heart, do a fancy two step around two very small blockages, then wire him up like a chicken in a poultry market but first, yeah, first take him off the machine that's keeping him alive and hope his sweet dear heart starts pumping on its own. Come on heart! You can do it heart! Then wire him shut like a canary in a pet store, sew him up and hope when he comes out of anesthesia he doesn't gag on the tube down his throat. Keep him in the hospital 4-7 days, feed him slop and teach him how to hold a heart - shaped pillow…how precious, tight against his chest every time he sneezes or coughs or god forbid laughs, because if he splits open the stitches that are tenuously holding the bones of his chest together then holy shit he'll be back in surgery again.

All this for two small blockages that the doctor says probably could be controlled by diet and exercise.

We stumble through the parking lot looking for our car. Crawl inside and turn on the A/C. Begin to eat the roast chicken I packed from home. Cucumber slices. Crackers. Mustard. Cold water.

We chew in silence.

So? I say.

I can't do that, he says.

Of course not, I say and we start the long drive home.

*Flooded with relief, we drive home with my hand on your heart, its steady reassuring beat.*

We fought so much in the beginning. That first Valentine's Day we were together I was insecure, needing more reassurance than you knew how to give, so unwilling to risk my heart that I gave you nothing while you gave me flowers and a card that said you would always love me.

*I saved that card. I have it still.*

Sometimes in my distress and mistrust, desperate to provoke a fight, I'd reach for the last unforgivable sign from you that you did not love me, and threaten to pull down the whole edifice of our life. I'd say we ought to divorce without meaning it, or wanting it, and then freeze in terror if you appeared to be considering it as an option.

*Your love cracked me open, tamed and disarmed me.*

You went to work on the island, became a building contractor so I could stay home and nurse our baby. You came back to me tired, covered in dust.

*I kissed you anyway. Your mouth tasted the same.*

When I looked up flights to Tahiti and then remembered we couldn't afford them,

*I loved you anyway.*

The only things we were ever certain of were our child and each other. The only constant was this holy crucible where we joined, me around you inside me.

Last night Richard unearthed a box of all the Valentines I've given him over the years. The ones I bought, and the ones I made when our daughter was young, red construction paper, stickers, glitter and glue, a picture of our family pasted inside. A stack of cards like a flip book of a heart slowly opening. Is this safe? What if he abandons me? Or dies like my father did when I was a child? *What if what if what if* giving way over time to gratitude and awe that such good fortune could befall us.

We have aged, been softened by illness, by loss and by heartbreak; we have grown wise enough to know that love that endures is worth cradling with both hands.

I'm still scrappy and hot tempered but I've mellowed with time. My scars have taught me that everything done without love will wound and disappoint me, and I have whispered a promise to spirit that I will not walk that road again.

This is the history of love written in cards, on the sand, on post-its and lipstick on the mirror. This is the story of choosing love over fear, and the sweet relief of surrender.

# Wild Ride

I COMMITTED TO MY MARRIAGE 36 years ago. I'd do it all over again.

The alternative: the whole mess of dating and the slow process of getting to know someone, of unfolding personal histories like bridge hands, offering small scenes from a long ago childhood like a box of miniature chocolates, each one with a different filling. Sea salt caramel for all the tears spilled. Creamy coconut for the milky maternal years, dark truffles for all the secrets too dense to bite into just yet.

So I am grateful to feel the same warm body next to mine as I fall asleep, listening to the rasp of the pages of his mystery turn against the sheets. Yet how many times have I wanted to say - could you please do that a little quieter? Could you please not tug on the blanket? Must you blow your nose so loud? But I don't, because I know death sits lightly on the edge of the bed in a sharkskin suit twirling his fedora, admiring his polished shoes.

He's listening. Maybe hoping I'll speak sharply to my beloved, not because death is cruel, he's not, but because he knows that part of the medicine he carries in the embroidered silk pouch around his neck is the fine powder of regret.

He waits and watches, his fingers always ready to sprinkle regret liberally like salt in soup, raining down upon the living, filling our mouths with bitter ash. If only. Why did I? I wish I hadn't.

So many ways for the heart to fold in on itself, all valleys and dark shadows, filled with why why why. Why me, why now, why is this the way it ends?

And that is the specter that keeps me steady during this storm that is committed love, this wild amusement park ride that is often not funny, just scary, just holding on, just making it past the next plunge into the dark tunnel, rising up again into pure clean air where we say, *oh finally*.

But it is never *finally*. There is no end to the wild ride, to the unpredictable nature of the next spin and dip. There's no saying when the wheel will get stuck and leave you dangling at the top, at the whim of the winds and the storm that is brewing, always brewing.

Perhaps it is knowing just how quickly death can rise from the end of the bed, stretch out his hand and

## THE RIPENING | Ripen

scoop up the last breath of my beloved. Perhaps it is constantly remembering that he carries the medicine of regret that keeps me steady, asking for the grace to learn patience, learn kindness, before it is too late.

Nancy London

# Word Salad

WHAT IF THERE'S SOMETHING wrong with my brain?
 This morning I said we lived in a *Jupiter* forest instead of *Juniper*. How I couldn't find the word *refund* yesterday, how it all became kind of fuzzy and foggy. How I tried to tell my friend Leslie about my daughter's dream of being an old woman with a gray braid and instead said gray beard. I try for a longer sentence with Richard and I don't even recognize some of the words that slink out of my mouth like sow bugs unearthed from under a rock.
 What if these lapses of mind and vocabulary are more than normal, whatever normal is.
 I remember how my hospice dementia patients spoke what we called word salad - a slurring sliding jumble of syllables, weird substitutions, one word for another, sort of close to the meaning but not really. I'd know she meant the *finish line* but she said the *flannel line* instead. Soon her mangled words began to sound

like the Beatles played backwards at the wrong speed. Looking at me with those huge baby doe eyes, begging, *I made sense didn't I? Please tell me I made sense.* I know just what you mean, I'd say and they'd beam at me, so relieved for one moment that their very worst fear was not true, that they were not sliding down a slick slope with no railings into a mess of black muck that would claim them like it did the tar baby.

But of course it was true and would be true until they were no longer able to produce words, their swallowing reflex shut down, their liquids thickened, their foods pureed and sanitized to a colorless lump not even a cat would sniff.

Last night at sunset, Richard and I walk under clouds of metallic gold and pink, and I want suddenly to demonstrate the old marching song from sleepaway camp. *Left, left, left my wife with 48 kids, right, right, right in the middle of the kitchen floor* but when I hop from left to right my foot catches on the uneven pavement and I fall hard on my hands and left knee. I am bruised, bleeding, weeping.

What's happening to me, I cry as Richard wraps his arms around me and leads me the rest of the way home.

I don't want to unravel, I cry into his shoulder. Don't let me unravel.

Is my mind unraveling like the unknitting of a fine sweater I could always count on to keep me warm? The fast brain, out - strategizing everyone at the speed of light. The neurons firing like an automatic rifle with the perfect retort, the perfect flash flood string of words to devastate, educate and elucidate.

Who will I be without her? Will I be a smiling old lady drooling off in the corner? So sweet, so sweet the dogs come around to make sure she is safe. She pats them but does not remember their names. No matter. One is black, one is tan with funny little short legs and a big appetite. She feeds them, even though that woman who she says is her daughter asks her not to, but it makes them so very very happy.

Nancy London

# Weary Warrior

My warrior princess found me in my pajamas, under the covers, watching bad TV.

Go away, I said. I've got a few health challenges I don't want to talk about and honestly, you're standing in my light.

She stretched out next to me, took a pillow without asking.

Tired? she asked, flipping the channel to a rerun of The Wire.

Yes. I was tired.

I've brought you something, she said.

Ice cream?

No honey. The photo album you left by the side of the road.

Well hell, I said. That's why I left it there.

She began flipping through pages.

Look, she said, and I looked.

There I was, twelve years old, my handsome sweet

daddy just dead.

Look what you're doing, she said.

I looked. With both hands I was heaving up a shield and strapping it across my chest.

Remember?

I did.

And here. She pointed to my mother marrying and marrying and marrying, each time pushing me further outside her home. See? she said. And I saw.

Bigger shield now, bigger muscles.

Oh and look here.

I saw my wild one, my teenager running scared and hungry through dark wet nights, daring anyone to approach. Closer, I'd whisper. I've got a surprise. The Japanese sword shaped like a claw that ripped open the hearts of my suitors so that I could taste their sorrow and grow strong. Stronger.

And here, a picture of me - a young woman, a feminist fool giving lectures on why women should leave their men. So ignorant of why two people cleave to each other and what it would cost to rip them apart.

Big strong warrior, she said, feeling my biceps, carrying that shield for so many years. So safe from wounding.

But you *were* wounded, she said, and showed me pictures of my lost babies, betrayals, loved ones gone, my mother's suicide, my brother's descent into madness.

Your shield didn't help you then, did it?

And now, she said, now you face challenges your rage and your wit cannot overcome. Your body ages and does not sing the way it used to. How will you do battle now? How will you travel through the desert of this time with no canteen, breaking open stones in search of water?

What good is your shield now?

I knew she was right. I had no strength left to fight, no will to slay the dragon, no map to guide me through the chaos of this new storyfield.

Fighting, winning the battle, meeting the challenge, overcoming the enemy, all of this yang when I was yearning for yin. My warrior, sweet girl with the sad tired eyes, needed rest. She'd battled patriarchy, misogyny, rapists, bullies. Liars, hustlers, thin gypsy thieves. She'd burned down cathedrals, been barefoot and broken, walked through the fire, been queen for a day.

Now I was weary, wanting only to learn kindness, patience and forgiveness.

Now I wanted to return from the depths with the old stories that speak of myth, of fog, of the courage to plunge from the cliffs of doubt. Stories about descent and renewal, and how to return with the magic spells to make my world new again, because the world as I knew it was already gone.

How shall I live? I asked her, and although I did not know her name, I knew she came bearing the flag of surrender. She had come from the land of know nothing, give everything, let your moan open the door.

This is how, she said. And she gave me the language the birds understood, that stopped coyotes on the dusty trail, caused them to turn, to raise their ears, to open their mouths and call *Sister*.

# Cherish Every Stupid Moment

How to mark this day? What to call it so that looking back I will remember what I did - not the mundane wash dishes, answer mail, prepare dinner, chop veggies kind of day. How do I mark the *before* so that when I look back I can see how sweet this day was, how innocent I was, compared to the next and the next, how unspeakably young I felt compared to the *after*, when I will have read the PET scan results arriving tomorrow.

I am waiting, waiting, for the sound of the gavel coming down on the block.

I do all kinds of things to deal with the anxiety of not knowing. I cook, repot my plants, organize my closet by color, barely manage my abject craving for sugar. I'm reading *Spy Secrets That Can Save Your Life,* and have made a list of emergency supplies - the obvious, like waterproof matches, flashlight, batteries and protein bars. But then there's duct tape, bolt cutters, a tactical spy pen with a sharp pointy end that doubles as a weapon, and a stack of one dollar bills so I can bribe my way out of the country. Why? Because this is what the far edge of coping looks like.

How do I breathe today, cherishing every stupid moment of not knowing, relishing every tick tock in this privileged land of wellness that may only last for one more day before the diagnosis, the phone call. This day as fragile and gorgeous as a soap bubble.

Look! I want to cry to Richard. Look how perfect this body I condemned for growing old but look! It is still whole today. Look at these plans I made for what to do this summer, foolish me with my road atlas, tracing the lines that lead from the desert across the country to warm beaches and ripe fruit. Look! I want to cry. Look at this life I thought was becoming lifeless, this home not big enough, too little of this or too much or that.

On this last day of not knowing can I ever again find fault with what has been given, with what I hold in my two hands, brimming over with blessings. The everything that pulses within me is so luminous, so full, so glorious, so fucking alive on this day of waiting, I know it can all turn to sand through open fingers, like music through the wind chimes signaling a storm.

This holy moment, this sacred yes, this now, this please I am on my knees asking for mercy, asking for good news or at least if that is too much to ask for, asking for the grace to roll the stone away and stand on my sturdy legs, my lover by my side, ask to be given if not good news, then given the heart and soul to endure.

Nancy London

# Slower, Funnier, Wiser

THE PET SCAN SHOWS there's nothing wrong with my brain, but the MRI says - well, maybe. So I give up trying to make sense of the results and walk outside into the courtyard where I am struck dumb by the beauty of the world. Sunlight as it crests the mountains flooding my garden, sweet as warm honey. Manna from the open palm of a loving presence.

I whistle to the small bird at the feeder, the one with the Mohawk haircut whose name I remember and then forget, who looks up from eating the seed I leave out.

Yes, hello she says, and thank you.

No, I whistle. Thank you.

No really, she sings. Thank you.

We whistle back and forth in this game that fills me with such happiness I feel close to levitating.

And this. When I see my husband across the room I think...now, here, this moment. Cherish him, for it changes, moves on, eclipses, passes. Open your heart and say yes to everything this moment has brought. The grief, the worry, the uncertainty, the relief.

Yes to the laughter that rises up when we talk of our child and how much fun it was to raise her.

Yes to all the losses and triumphs, the face down in the mud failures, the brokenhearted moments of sickness and worry, the death of friends and family we will always miss, the ones we call out to in our dreams... Wait! I have one last thing to say. But really the one last thing is yes and yes and yes and thank you and I love you and I would do it all over again.

And now darling, bringer of joy and hot water bottles, tea and night time pills, it is the two of us again after so many years. And now my beloved, tender as spring rain, patient as the tides, it is us alone again but older now, slower, funnier, wiser I suppose, but definitely older. We hold hands when we walk. You rub my feet when we watch movies. You scratch my back.

We are coming upon the winter of our time together, and while I have no fear of dying, I cannot imagine for one small moment living without the warmth of your sun, the grounding of your strong body, your hands that assure me in the middle of the night that all is well. The silly songs you sing to the dog, the stir fry, the curries, the fragrance of your love that has nourished me all these long lovely years.

I wake and follow the smell of coffee into the kitchen, fold myself into your lap, nuzzle the warm sleep still caught in the folds of your neck. Breathe you in as if you are life itself. Breathe out and say, I am so glad you're here.

Nancy London

# The New Story

THE NEW STORY: slower. Step here, not there. Watch the path, not the wandering thought. Whatever you think you did wrong, it's already done. The toast has already burned and been scraped into the compost. The too hot iron has already left its scorch mark on your new silk shirt. The new story: leave regrets like an old sofa that smells of cat pee by the side of the road for garbage collection day.

Guess what? I whisper. Whatever you're fretting about? It's already happened. Let go the worry, the endless fear that you have harmed someone with your careless tongue. Guess what? You've already said it. Make amends. If they're dead, light a candle and move on.

Time is a river and you are standing on the shore. Wait. Did I remember my scarf? An extra pair of socks? Too late. You've already packed. The train is tooting, the river is flowing. Jump onto the escalator if you cannot walk, but move. Time is moving, the river is moving, and you must move too. Place your foot here and not there. If you do not look you will stumble, and you now know that leads to more broken bones and endless limping.

The new story is here, in the present. 'The present has no opposite"* but the future and past pair up, tweedle dee and tweedle dum, tipping this way, tipping back again. What if I did something wrong, what if it doesn't work out, who will I become, who am I leaving behind? The endless seesaw, fretting away the hours while the angels dance on the balance point.

Here is the new story: this moment contains all of eternity. Not holy shit I blew it, or I won't know what to do when the next moment arrives or the next or the next, because I don't know if there will be a next, or if there will be the sudden explosion in my brain that will silence these worries forever, or if the plane will sputter and plunge as I fly home to my husband who waits patiently for me.

There is only here. Step carefully. This moment will last forever, will carry me into the arms of the Beloved if I can stay present, chanting softly *here here here* as I walk, dry the dishes, get ready for bed. *Here* as I wake, stretch, put water on to boil. *Here* as I dress, cook breakfast, sit down to write.

Put one foot down. Follow with the other. Take a breath, exhale, say *here*. It is the only safety net, the only sanctuary, the only place to call home.

* quote from *"Not Poems: Moments of Awareness"*
  page 1, by Donna Thomson

# Sanctuary

To celebrate our first night together 36 years ago, Richard surprised me with new cotton sheets…jungle cats leaping across a tropical rain forest, and when I told my girlfriend, all she said was *Keep him.*

Cool cotton sheets in the summer, thick flannel sheets in the winter, the colors and fabrics changing with the seasons here in the high desert but always the white down comforter because no matter the season the nights grow cold.

Our bed is where we learned to read the language of our bodies. Touch me here like this. Slower. Does this feel good? More. And always laughter, two young lovers on a ship that was our bed sailing out onto the sea of marriage. Our hands reaching for each other in the dark, mine cold, his always warm, the way I stole his body heat, the way he gave it gladly.

Our bed with our baby sleeping between us, so afraid we would roll over and crush her. Our bed with the window open to the sea and the lullaby of water on stone.

Our bed where we waited past her curfew. Where is she? Is she safe? Shall we call the police? Moving away from each other to catch a breeze during that hot summer of her new driver's license, the cotton sheets damp, the air heavy. Where is she? Is she safe?

Our bed where he watched over me in illness and a sudden diagnosis that frightened us as we rode out that wave in our bed.

Floating through time and space in our bed, fingers touching, maybe spooning if it's snowing, snuggled under a cloud of grey flannel, and then she is safe and she is gone off to her own bed and her own mate.

And still we reach for each other, still strip down in the heat and the freezing cold to find each other again, trace the outline of aging flesh, adore the scars, the place where the knife carved my breast, where the bone in my foot grew back misaligned.

We float out to sea in our bed and I follow the moon as it rises and falls through the bedroom window. The nights it is full she comes in without being asked and bathes us in silver cool light, shines on us as we lie together moon cycle after moon cycle, knowing our girl is safe, knowing we are aging, have aged, knowing one night one of us will reach across the bed and there will be space, just space across the vast deck of the ocean liner that is tugging us out to sea, that has picked up our small vessel and is leading us further and further out onto a current where there is no going back, just forward towards a place of sanctuary and stillness, of light so blinding, of love so total that to reach out a hand is to be met by the Beloved, always waiting just beyond the next wave, ready to catch the solitary lover who is drowning in despair, ready to rock us and sing us the lullaby we remember from home.

Nancy London

# Dancing to the End of Time

THERE IS AN ENDLESS list of what I have resisted.

I resisted thinking about how to start a career when I graduated from college and instead, ended up tuning pianos for a living.

*That's* what you're doing with a college education? my mother asked.

Yep. For the moment that's what I was doing.

I resisted playing the piano after years of professional training until a gypsy lover with a piano in his velvet lined van placed my fingers back on the sound of my soul. E minor, A minor, the melodies from the old country pouring out of me, no more resistance.

I resisted marriage. I knew I'd have to curb my wild, my free, my all - night gone and kohl rimmed eyes. I married a man who let me out on a long rope and then waited for me to tug. Please reel me back in, I signaled. I've had enough.

I have resisted the endless march of time, Chronos on

a horse galloping at mad speed, tearing time from the calendar of my life. Faster, he yells to his horse while I struggle against the wind, fall to my knees, begging. Slow down, I cry. Slow down. Too fast. Too many things left undone, but he rides faster, kicking up the dust that blurs the rising moon.

So many families that are no more. Mother father brothers sisters lovers friends, my old aunties and uncles, the ones who pulled quarters out of my ear, tickled me, made me laugh, looked out for me after my father died, all memorialized in a snow globe on a summer night when the fireflies lit up the sky with their Morse code. Blink. Blinkblink. Time is running out. And then all of them saddled to the back of the galloping black horse down an overgrown path where I could not follow.

I want to know where Chronos has taken them. And when the wind blows their memories in the window and I am wrapped in longing, I want to know where to find them again.

It is always morning. It is always time for bed. Toothbrush coffee cup shopping list cedar closet winter boots flip flops sunscreen wool coat endless endless the race to catch up with Chronos who is always, will always be out of reach with a wild *Yeehah* over his shoulder.

But Kairos. She comes to me and says: child, come

dance into the timeless circle with me. That is where they have gone. Beyond the straight line and sculpted hedges is where you will find them. Reach up and leave your handprint on the sky. Breathe out and leave your prayers on the ground. Let yourself be broken open and shaken by the great forces of the universe.

If you stop resisting, if you stop clinging and digging your heels in the dirt, tearing page after page off of what remains of your life, if you stop endlessly counting how many years left with your beloved, how many left to see your child in her faraway land, if you let go we will catch you and dance you out into the wild where the old ones dance.

Look. Sun rises and flowers open. The birds come and the soil warms. Look. Moonrise and the nightshades bloom. The moths dance and the roots rest. Look again. The sun rises. Do you see the round, the ripe, the everlasting cycles she asks, taking my hand and leading me onto the dance floor.

She dances me in a spiral that began where I was born. We spiral up and out towards the light, towards the one pure light that knows no time, that is outside of time and that waits in oneness with all the time in the world. We are dancing towards the light that is another name for timeless, for once upon a time, a light that is another name for love.

*Dancing to the End of Time*

Nancy London

# Prayers for the Dead

OH SWEET MERCY they all showed up today, as if I had sent out celestial engraved invitations. Ms. London, Nanny, Nan, or fancy pants Nance to some of you, requests your presence tonight on Yom Kippur, the holiest night of the year when we stand before the One Great Spirit and ask to be forgiven for our failures to the living and to the dead. She will light candles and honor your memory, still a blaze in her heart. She will recite the *Kol Nidre*, the prayer for the dead, as best she can, given how long it has been since she last spoke Hebrew, and call you forth alive and well in your flimsy gossamer garments.

And then my brother appears and gives me his crooked Elvis smile, rolling a cigarette, and I cry to see him so whole. What is there to ask of him? That he forgives me for not having been strong enough glue him back together as he tumbled into darkness, shattered into madness and self-destruction?

I reach out and touch his face. I miss you, I say. I miss your crappy jokes and how no one else knows what hell it was to live with Mom. I miss you.

And then my father emerges, and he's radiant and distant as he always was. This is your night, Pop, I joke. Want to dance? But instead, he folds me against his chest and lets me cry until the snot runs down his beautifully pressed white shirt. Who the hell is doing your laundry? I ask but it's a feeble attempt at humor to deflect my grief, because all these years all these years all these years. And he brings me to the water's edge and says, this is why you dream of water. It's where we meet. Where we will always meet. He winks at me. Straight on till morning, darlin'. Straight on till morning.

There is someone moving out of the shadows. He is an old man, long white beard, black robe, yarmulke on his head. He looks at me with such compassion, such abiding love, I understand immediately that he is my great grandfather, the rabbi of the village that was destroyed, everyone and everything reduced to fire and ash in the pogroms.

He puts his cold hand in mine and on this night when the dead are dancing, when the candles are flickering and the owls are hooting, this night when the moon is struggling against gravity because she too wants to fall to the ground and weep with me for the dead who are assembled, weep for the ancestors standing even further back in the shadows, unnamed but remembered, on this night I honor them with my hot tears, the ancient ones who survived long enough to make my life possible.

The dreamscape is crowded with all my beloveds, all the ones I yearn to share a meal with again. And then my mother Rosie enters center stage, her gold high heels clicking across the tile, and of course her Joy perfume and we fall on each other weeping, saying I'm sorry. I love you. Please forgive me.

I ask for a sign to bring back from this vision so that they will not be gone but always with me, always living and dying and living and dying. And then there is a hand rolled cigarette in the driveway and none of us smokes, and some of the coffee ice cream, my brother's favorite, has been hacked away with a spoon, and another dreamtime dive into the ocean, another adventure with my father, and the always heartbreak that keeps him close to me.

They are all with me. I see that now.

And then holy of holy. The sound of my own high heel boots this morning on the tile. Mama!

# Part Five

## HARVEST

Nancy London

# Time and the River

LISTEN. THIS IS A STORY about time running forwards and backwards, like a river when the currents are pushed upstream away from the sea, the fish holding to their course, carried closer to where they began.

This is a story about time and the changes it brought to the daughter we hadn't seen in almost three years of international travel bans imposed by covid.

This is a story about flying forward in time, about two days Richard and I spent in airports and cramped airplane seats watching sixteen hours of bad movies to see the child now grown into the woman mated and rooted in a faraway land we had to travel forward to see again.

This is the story of the old woman who appeared in my daughter's kitchen in the early morning, the big windows looking out onto the fog, drifting like lace, like cobwebs, covering then revealing the mountain on the far side of the meadow.

Who are you? I asked. What do you want?

I am who I have always been, she said quietly. I have been called to help you through this time of change.

I did not need to ask what was changing. My child had changed into a woman, into an eagle, into a wild spirit roaming her farm, swimming in fast running waters. My child had moved backwards and disappeared into the mist of memory and forward into a time beyond my time.

This is the story of the old woman who stood next to me as I made my way tentatively over uneven terrain, hesitant, aware of the fragility of my bones.

Sit, she said, and contemplate what comes next. See where the river will take you if you let go, if you let the river cool your fevers of desire and attachment. Sit and see what will be left.

What are you losing? she asked me. What parts of yourself no longer serve you as you allow this transformation to work itself through and upon you? What is dying and what is being born and can you see in the dark? Can you trust the chrysalis to dissolve you into nothingness and emerge with fresh wings back into the light?

I was a maiden yearning for a child to fill my belly, then a mother with milk overflowing, now a woman blessing a child who has grown beyond my reach.

I am an aging woman cutting the cord, letting go and letting the river take me past curves and over currents into rapids and onto stretches of clear calm blue. A salmon, a dolphin, a turtle finding the sand of home and resting, finally resting, drifting on a moonless night out onto dark waters, stripped down to my skin, phosphorescing under the endless bright stars, letting the current drag something new from the shells and discarded skins left behind.

You will be ripped apart and reassembled, she said. Destroyed and made whole again by loss and illness, death and despair, grief as deep and pure as a bottomless well.

Do not waste your pain, she said.

If we allow our hearts to break, the threads connecting us deep into the best of ourselves will weave us back into the world as the river flows backwards into our memories, where we hold those we have lost tenderly as a hummingbird egg, where we cherish what once was. And if we allow time and the river to move us forward into the unknown, where change is another name for loss, we will be sustained by the steady never changing power of love.

Listen. This is the story of the river that washes us clean of any backwards notion of the shame we have carried this long, this far, then moves us forward, free of any doubt that we are gifted, that what we say matters, that we are loved by spirit beyond our understanding, that it is safe, it is time in this time of change, to reclaim our lives with both hands, redeem our right to shine, to share our love with a full heart, a sorrowing and joyful heart, a heart that yearns to be of service to a broken world.

Listen.

THE RIPENING |

# No More Fixing

WHEN I WAS A BABY they called me Happy.

Happy to sit in my playpen with a soft ripe banana. Happy to be kissed by the sun. Happy happy to have everyone around me smile when I smiled. Mommy, Daddy, everyone so happy to see Happy smile.

And now here at the end and the beginning, I am happy again. Happy with simple things. Happy with the love of my husband, daughter, friends and extended family. Happy to have survived the long dark road I traveled.

I want to open my heart and spill out the song I brought home. Listen. It's in the key of E minor. I carried their grief back - my mother's, my brother's. I dug a small hole in my garden under the flowering apple tree. I buried their sorrow and it freed me.

I could not fix them. I could not fix my father who died too young, weary of trying to be a success, leaving us to fight and bite and claw our way out of hell. I could not fix my brother, the dark demons that chased him down and devoured him. I could not place my warm hands on my mother's beating heart and give her the gift of wanting. Wanting to be kind, to be loved, to be alive.

This may not sound like much, but it is everything. When I'm not fixing others, I'm happy. Puttering in the garden, writing, cooking, dancing, feeding the birds. The quieter I get, the easier it is to forgive myself for everyone I could not fix.

I did not know any better. I did my best.

The list of what I can fix is so small. Fix the hurts I inflict on others when I'm angry, fix the ways I hurt myself when I am scared and empty. Crawl inside the folds of my brain with a tiny screwdriver and fix the ways I see the Other as the Enemy. Fix my list of priorities so that kindness wins out over speed, silence over how right I think I am.

Fix me and I fix the world.

I've put down my tools. I'm learning to let things be, to let silence fall, to let touch speak. If I listen, I can hear the dance at the edge of the clearing. All those I have loved are celebrating my homecoming. They've waited so patiently for me to understand there is no fixing, just the opening to the grace at the heart of the world where there is joy and misery, hardship and triumph, to the grief that breaks us and the love that puts us back together again, where everything is waiting to be embraced by someone who has given up fixing.

Nancy London

# I Wish Someone Had Told Me

I WISH SOMEONE HAD told me that time is elastic, a trickster, flowing as slow as the muddy stretches of the Chama River on a hot August day, then a raging whitewater avalanche of current, tumbling at torrential speed over rocks. I wish someone had told me that all those years I was raising a family, days blurring into nights blurring into dawn and sinking down into dusk again, that all those meals scraped off plates and dishes washed, would lead to this moment, when doors close on youth.

I wish someone had told me that my hearing and eyesight would dim, and that these changes would happen gradually, sneak up on me like a cat looking for a rub, like a breeze gathering outside an open window. Like clouds massing for a storm.

I wish someone had told me that I would feel diminished by these losses. I wish I had known to bless my younger self and all she was capable of seeing and hearing.

I wish someone had told me that regret sits lightly on the heart like a bird in the pear tree, that grief can whisper as well as wail, and that sorrow can find no words to tell you what she is feeling.

I wish someone had told me that caring for myself wasn't selfish, that saying no had the blessings of spring rain and midnight thunder, and that withdrawing into silence was where I would find renewal.

I wish someone had told me that most of my schemes would burn up like kindling and instead, that my life would unfold petal by petal, sweet as a juicy ripe peach.

I wish someone had told me that the heart is meant to be broken, and I no longer needed to be saved from love.

I wish I had known that I would come to love the man I married in ways tender as a bruise on fruit.

I wish someone had told me I would regret not having asked my grandmothers about their journeys from Odessa, Polynya, Kyiv, leaving mothers and fathers, brothers and sisters, aunties uncles dogs cows crops the river the town, all gone up in flames, all left behind to start a new life here on this soil. I wish someone had told me I would need them to tell me how to age with grace and gratitude, how to turn losses and regrets towards a distant shore where a radiant spirit opens her arms like a benevolent mother, where the heart grows wider and brighter as the body declines.

I wish someone had told me that prayer is the fuel I would need to keep my faith burning.

Change is upon me and it is coming swiftly, a dark horse riding through the night, and when the full moon wakes me I hear the relentless hoof beats of time and tide and the turning of the seasons sweeping me along, like the leaves that fall in autumn when the wind shakes the trees. Golden aspens surrendering with a grace I can only aspire to, sure that when they fall it is not the end, that there is more, much more happening beneath the ground, a life process that will slowly erode the known shape, break down the parts, separate leaf and stem, bone and muscle, transformed into something unimaginable, something that sparkles and shimmers, glows in the dark, gives off light like a bioluminescent sea creature.

Can you hear us? they call. Come closer. You are in the cocoon, cozy in the warm dark, sleeping the sleep of the child who knows not what awaits her, but trust us, they say. When the time comes the transformation will be complete.

And then. And then you will be sustained by the radiant emptiness, where love and suffering, light and shadow, pain and joy become as one, a comfort and a blessing as you make your way home.

Nancy London

# Epilogue: Old Age Comes Happy

HAPPY OLD AGE IS COMING on bare feet. She is grinning, her basket overflowing with flowers and grapes. She lives in a new land, fertile green, dappled with new birdsong and fresh smells. She cannot stop marveling at the soil, rich and black and happy to welcome seed and rain.

Old age comes happy with her child by her side, now grown and full of belly, carrying a child of her own, the circle finally complete. The wailing ancestors who stood on the shore as the great ships pulled out with their beloved children in steerage below deck, huddled together in flight and fright, the mothers who never saw their children again, they are now appeased.

Happy old age comes on bare feet whistling off key, her back tooth missing, her eyesight dimming, the limp from the break that never healed, the wounds, the scars, the black and blues that faded out like the last chord of a concert, all of it running together like watercolors to blur and make a new scene.

If you squint you can see her holding out her arms for a baby that has not yet arrived, building a shelter with stone not yet all gathered. This is the song she is whistling, the song of readying, the slow chug of the train pulling out of the station, the deep rumble of the plane, the motorcycle, the souped up car, the thrum between the legs that says readiness is all, we are readying as the seasons turn and the cycles begin again.

We are readying.

# Acknowledgements

So much love and gratitude to the following:

To my brilliant writing teacher Laura Lentz whose Tuesday writing group provided the space for me to write many of the essays in this book. She brings her generous heart, inspiration, poetry, prose and an unwavering belief that our stories have the power to change the world.

To the Tuesday Trusted Troubadours: Donna, Elissa, Erika, Francine, Joia, Katrina, Lee, Margaret, the other Nancy, Tammra and Verena, such gratitude for the years we have been writing our way through illness, loss, heartbreak and joy. Bottomless love for our sacred circle.

Thank you to Donna Orbach, friend and fearless editor, who provided her usual penetrating feedback – time given generously to my book when she should have been working on her own.

Gratitude again and always to Laura Lentz who made time to read these essays, even when her grandson was doing wheelies on his tricycle in her office.

To Laura Davis with love for friendship, fertile collaborations, her careful reading of an early draft, and for knowing about daughters who live far away.

Love and gratitude to Leslie Nathanson not only for being an early reader, but for deepest soul food friendship all these long years.

To Marta Townsend who helped me see my way clear to writing a better book when I wanted to give up.

To all the Facebook readers who kept asking when I was going to publish a collection of my essays – thank you for the encouragement and for so many kind words. It was exactly the nudge I needed.

Thank you to Limor Farber whose immense talent designed this book and its luscious cover.

To my daughter Sasha and her partner Rhys who poured their love and sweat into Green Goddess Farm, life overflowing and regenerating in abundance. You inspire me every day.

And finally endless love and gratitude to my husband Richard, heart of my heart, whose steady love and care have been the center of my life for 36 years. Thank you for our daughter, for your deep wellspring of kindness and forgiveness, for early morning laughter and late night conversation, for your bright brilliant paintings (richardwelkerart.com), and the fabulous meals you conjure when I'd swear there was nothing in the fridge. None of this is possible without you. No matter where we are, you are my safe place, my home.

# About the Author

Nancy London is the author of *Hot Flashes, Warm Bottles: First-Time Mothers over Forty* and one of the original authors of *Our Bodies, Ourselves.* She holds a master's degree in social work, and for more than a decade was part of a hospice team. She lives in Santa Fe, New Mexico with her husband of 36 years, where she is a freelance writer and editor, and has a private practice specializing in grief support.

Learn more about Nancy at **nancylondonwriter.com**

Printed in Great Britain
by Amazon